Heterogeneity in Macroeconomics and its Implications for Monetary Policy

Fabian Schnell

Heterogeneity in Macroeconomics and its Implications for Monetary Policy

With a foreword by Prof. Dr. Reto Föllmi

Springer Gabler

Fabian Schnell
Universität St. Gallen
St. Gallen, Switzerland

Dissertation, University of St. Gallen, Switzerland, 2014

ISBN 978-3-658-09730-1 ISBN 978-3-658-09731-8 (eBook)
DOI 10.1007/978-3-658-09731-8

Library of Congress Control Number: 2015937603

Springer Gabler

Printed on acid-free paper

Springer Gabler is a brand of Springer Fachmedien Wiesbaden
Springer Fachmedien Wiesbaden is part of Springer Science+Business Media
(www.springer.com)

Foreword

The role that monetary policy plays in the real economy has been discussed for a long time in economics. The expansionary and non-orthodox monetary measures to fight the adverse consequences of the Great recession have reignited the interest into these questions. Monetary policy affects business cycles because the increased liquidity provided by the central bank does not immediately raise prices. What we still do not know precisely how much time this price adjustment needs and through which channels it operates. Fabian Schnell's book provides a substantial contribution to a better understanding how business cycles evolve.

In a first part, Fabian Schnell analyzes the macroeconomic effects of the low real interest rates we see today. The relevance of the topic could not be more obvious. The chapter speaks to an ongoing policy debate on the consequences of the present low-interest policy. There is already a broad literature on the short-run consequences of a zero interest rate environment but there is, surprisingly, little research on its medium- and long-run consequences. The data from inflation-protected bonds indeed show that US real interest rates for different yield lengths have experienced a secular downturn since the beginning of the Great recession in 2009.

The author makes the empirically relevant assumption that firms differ in productivity. Firms' heterogeneity, their creation and destruction processes have only recently gained attention in the literature. These mechanisms are central to understand the medium-run impact of low interest rates. In such an environment, unproductive firms may stay in the market which is detrimental to aggregate productivity since capital stays in the unproductive firms and is not reallocated to the innovative ones. Hence, there is a trade-off between short-run stabilization and the recovery of the economy in the medium-run. Interestingly and paradoxically, the central bank should tighten the interest rate in reaction to a negative demand shock. Intuitively, lower real interest rates would be prolonging the recovery, because lax monetary conditions allow more low-productive firms to stay in the market and therefore decrease the aggregate productivity level. These insights make the success of further monetary quantitative easing highly questionable.

The second part of the book then scrutinizes the cornerstone of the monetary transmission mechanism: how firms adjust their prices. For this aim, the Swiss sectoral CPI for 4 sectors is used where individual prices can be observed. The panel consists of more than 300'000 observations between 1993 and 2012. Different from other price data sets used in the literature (such as the US CPI), firms stay for a long period in the sample which effectively allows to calculate sample means and higher moments of the distribution. It turns out that firm-specific state-dependent variables are most crucial to understand the pricing decision. In particular, firms at the lower end of the price spectrum use exogenous cost shocks such as tax increases to raise their prices disproportionally. Again, the individual behavior of the firm is crucial to understand macroeconomic price fluctuations.

The thesis provides new insights on the really "big" questions of macroeconomics. As all serious and good research, it offers many answers and new insights but raises at the same new questions. The book improves our understanding of the complex interaction of monetary conditions and the macroeconomy at times and circumstances when it is needed most.

St. Gallen, January 2015
Prof. Dr. Reto Föllmi

Acknowledgments

Writing this dissertation has been a rewarding, intellectually stimulating experience as well as a tough journey from time to time. Finally completing this journey is therefore a wonderful moment. I am indebted to all the people without whose support this project would never have been possible, and I am glad to have now the opportunity to thank them.

First, I am very grateful to my supervisor, Reto Föllmi. Although I had been working outside of the university, he accepted me as his doctoral student and was convinced of the merit of my research ideas from the beginning, likely even more convinced than I was. Subsequently, he also hired me as his research and teaching assistant. Reto's encouragement and support have always been important and have been a source of motivation. Despite being my academic role model, Reto has also become a good friend in recent years.

Furthermore, I would like to thank Peter Kugler, who fortunately agreed to be my co-referee, as well as the other two members of my committee, Francesco Audrino and Guido Cozzi, for their helpful comments. I am generally very indebted to Jörg Baumberger, who always inspired me as a teacher and in many discussions about economics. To work for him as an assistant during my master's studies actually encouraged me to pursue a Ph.D.

Second, and just as important, I would like to thank Ruedi Minsch and economiesuisse for all the support and flexibility that I have benefited from as your employee. Discussions regarding macroeconomics with Ruedi have often provided the necessary background for many of my research ideas. I am thankful to my entire team, Stefan Vannoni, Fridolin Marty, Philipp Bauer and Ines Rosenthal, as well as to all my other colleagues at economiesuisse for their patience and support. The same holds, of course, for all collaborators at the SIAW institute, particularly Irene Fensore, Isabel Martinez, Stefan Legge and Lukas Schmid, as well as the good souls of the institute, Gabriela Schmid and Michèle Klarer.

During my journey toward the Ph.D., I have met many new people sharing the same path and have profited from various economics-related discussions with these individuals. Without being able to list them all, I want to mention Tanja Artiga, Johannes Fritz, Florian Habermacher, Luzia Halter, Florian Landis, Jürg Müller, Jörg Schläpfer, Silvio Sticher and Carlo Strub. Additionally, I want to thank all my other friends who tolerated my crises and always supported me, especially Brenda Mäder, Alain Schreiner, Angela Eisenhut, André Fröhlich, Daniel Leuthard, Daniel Scherrer, Jürg Sandmeier, Silvan Amberg, Fabian Krek, Géraldine Schreiner, Thomas Albert, Jérôme Weber, Matthias Gartenmann, Jan Schumacher, Mario Senn, and of course Rafael Plessow. A special thank is dedicated to Darius Stuker for his friendship and his company over the past 15 years.

Without the support of my family, it would never have been possible to pursue all of my academic studies. This statement especially holds true for my parents, Barbara and Herbert Schnell, to whom I am deeply indebted not only for moral and financial support but also for giving me the right encouragement at the right time, especially during my youth. I will always be thankful for everything you have done for me. Furthermore, I strongly appreciate the support I enjoyed from my sisters, Nicole and Natascha, and their families. My thankfulness is also owed to the Thomann family for welcoming and supporting me.

Finally, I want to thank Fabienne Thomann for all her love, patience and encouragement, but especially for always understanding when I was absorbed in my own world of economic models. Without her unconditional support, especially during several small crises that I experienced, I would probably have never finished this project. Thank you!

Zurich, November 2014
Fabian Schnell

Contents

Abstract

This dissertation contributes to the growing literature addressing firm heterogeneity in macroeconomic research by focusing on the associated implications for monetary policy. Two theoretical models are developed that show new potential effects of heterogeneous productivity across firms on macroeconomic dynamics. The first model indicates that monetary policy, by influencing real interest rates, can distort the allocation of production resources across firms in the medium-run and therefore potentially delay economic recovery after a negative macroeconomic shock. The second model introduces a new amplification mechanism of exogenous technology shocks based on endogenous firm entry and heterogeneous productivity. Increasing competition after a positive shock forces less productive firms to leave the market, leading to higher a average productivity. This development, in turn, decreases the desirability of market entry. Depending on the dominating of these two effects, the model implies an acceleration or a deceleration effect. Moreover, monetary policy can influence this channel as it has an impact on firms' production costs but also on the costs of market entry. In the empirical part of the dissertation, the price setting behavior of firms is analyzed. It is shown that time-dependent, relative to state-dependent, factors play a small role with respect to the probability and the size of a price change. Furthermore, for the firms in the data set (non-tradable services), an appreciation of the Swiss franc leads to an increase in the probability of a positive price change and, to a lesser extent, in the size of price changes. Singling out one policy measure, it can be shown that an increase in the VAT is over-proportionally reflected in prices, although the costs of the concerned producers increase only proportionally due to the deductibility of input costs. All these findings can be of particular relevance to monetary policy.

Zusammenfassung

Diese Dissertation beschäftigt sich mit den makroökonomischen Konsequenzen der Annahme heterogener Firmen. Die geldpolitischen Implikationen stehen dabei im Vordergrund. In den ersten beiden, theoretisch ausgerichteten Kapiteln liegt der Fokus auf der Tatsache, dass Firmen unterschiedlich produktiv sind. Anhand eines entsprechenden Modells wird aufgezeigt, dass Geldpolitik, durch die Beeinflussung von Realzinsen, die Allokation von Ressourcen mittelfristig verzerren und damit die wirtschaftliche Erholung nach einer Rezession verzögern kann. Dies liegt daran, dass sich relativ unproduktive Firmen aufgrund der günstigen Refinanzierung im Markt halten können. Das zweite Modell legt den Fokus auf die kurzfristigen Implikationen unterschiedlicher Produktivität und zeigt einen Verstärkungsmechanismus von Technologieschocks. Erhöhter Wettbewerb nach einem positiven Schock zwingt relativ unproduktive Unternehmen aus dem Markt auszutreten, was die Durchschnittsproduktivität erhöht. Allerdings senkt dies auch die Attraktivität des Markteintritts, da eine Firma nun relativ produktiver sein muss, um Gewinn zu erwirtschaften. Dominiert der erste Effekt, ergibt sich ein Verstärkungsmechanismus. Das dritte Kapitel untersucht empirisch das Preissetzungsverhalten von Firmen. Es zeigt sich, dass zeitbezogene Faktoren (z.B. Zeitspanne zwischen Preisänderungen) einen kleineren Einfluss auf Wahrscheinlichkeit und Ausmass einer Preisänderung haben, als situationsbezogene (z.B. relative Marktposition). Eine Aufwertung des Schweizer Frankens führt bei den untersuchten Firmen (nicht-handelbare Dienstleistungen) zu höheren Preisen. Schliesslich zeigt sich, dass sich eine Erhöhung der MwSt. überproportional in der Anpassung der Preise niederschlägt, obwohl die Kosten, aufgrund der Abzugsmöglichkeit von Vorleistungen, nur proportional steigen. Alle diese Resultate sind relevant für die Geldpolitik.

List of Figures

List of Tables

1 Introduction: Heterogeneity and Macroeconomics

Macroeconomic research, by its definition, analyzes the behavior of the aggregated economy. At a first glance, it seems therefore a reasonable simplification to assume the presence of individually optimizing but representative agents (consumers, producers, governments, central banks, etc.) when developing respective models. However, we know from many empirical analyses that economic agents in fact differ in many aspects. As noted by Guvenen (2011), there are two reasons why economists might want to include this heterogeneity among agents in their models. First, they may want to study cross-sectional or distributional issues. Questions about distribution are not only important to understand why income or wealth inequality exist and rise in many industrialized economies. They are also relevant to the distributional consequences of several policy measures and to determine optimal tax policies. Second, heterogeneity can have an impact on aggregated outcomes, i.e., relying on a representative individual, assuming that the sum of the choices of several individuals is mathematically equivalent to the behavior of one average individual, might ignore relevant economic mechanisms. This is, for example, the case when insurance markets for consumers against individual idiosyncratic shocks are incomplete.[1]

This dissertation also focuses on the relevance of heterogeneity for macroeconomic aggregates, particularly with respect to heterogeneity in the production sector. Jovanovic (1982) is most likely the first to detect the potential relevance of the fact that firms substantially differ with respect to their size and productivity.

[1]See, for example, Aiyagari (1994).

Based on this work, Hopenhayn (1992) develops a tractable framework to consider heterogeneity across firms in macroeconomic models. Although this framework is used in several macroeconomic applications thereafter (e.g., by Hopenhayn and Rogerson (1993)), the actual breakthrough of the conception came with the so-called "new" new trade theory developed by Melitz (2003). This theory postulates that exposure to trade will only allow the most productive firms to export and, at the same time, forces the least productive firms to exit the market, leading to higher productivity in the aggregated economy, i.e., a more productive use of resources and an increase in welfare. Melitz' conception can be seen as a paradigm shift that is today, as Helpman (2006) notes, especially dominating in the literature on international trade and foreign direct investments.

Nevertheless, firm heterogeneity and the dynamic of firms' entry and exit play an increasingly important role in other areas of macroeconomic research, such as the business cycle (e.g., Bilbiie et al. (2012)) and the growth literature (e.g., Atkeson and Kehoe (2007)). This dissertation mainly concentrates on the implications of and for monetary policy from a theoretical but also an empirical point of view. The theoretical part, by using the work of Hopenhayn (1992) and Melitz (2003), contains on the one hand a medium-run perspective, where it is assumed that the central bank can influence real interest rates, and on the other hand a short-run perspective, where the central bank has an impact on firms' entry and exit decisions via the nominal cost structure. The empirical part uses micro price data to describe which factors influence the price setting behavior of individual firms. This analysis is of particular interest to central banks regarding inflation forecasts and with respect to the impact that monetary policy has on the price setting behavior.

The second chapter focuses on the mentioned medium-run effects. The "medium-run" in this context describes a state of the economy with flexible prices but sluggish capital stock or input shares. The motivation for this chapter lies in the long time-period of low real interest rates that we can observe in many industrialized countries over the last few years and that is mainly induced by the respective central banks. Despite these lax monetary conditions, most concerned countries (e.g., the US or the Euro area) are still growing below potential. Following these observations, we develop a model in which real interest rates that are too low hinder the economic recovery, as these interest rates allow relatively unproductive firms to stay in the market and bind economic resources (as in the Melitz (2003) framework without opening to trade). This dynamic implies that in the medium-run, monetary policy should seek, to push economic recovery, rather to increase interest rates after a negative macroeconomic shock to induce a reallocation of production factors to more productive firms. It is also shown that this dynamic entails a trade-off between the short-run and medium-run preferences of the central bank. The optimal policy from a welfare perspective, however, depends on the long-run interest rate (which is given by the discount factor of the households) relative to the welfare-maximizing interest rate because of the preference for variety in the model, i.e., under certain circumstances, individuals prefer to keep a greater variety instead of having a higher aggregated output. As the analysis is purely theoretical, a main focus of the chapter lies in the proof of the existence and uniqueness of the equilibrium in the described economy with the mentioned conditions.

In the third chapter, we focus on the implications of firms' entry and exit and productivity heterogeneity in a classical new Keynesian short-run framework. Of note, it is shown that these features together can induce a new channel for the amplification mechanism of exogenous technology shocks. As is normally the case in this class of models, economic expansion leads to higher entry rates and, therefore, increasing competition. However, due to productivity heterogeneity, this gives rise to a new channel. On the one hand, an individual firm must, due to the increased competition, be relatively more productive to stay in the market, which makes market entry less attractive but leads to an increase in economy-wide average productivity. On the other hand, this higher average productivity decreases the costs of market entry. Depending on which of these two effects dominate, the model implies an acceleration or a deceleration effect (because of the first mentioned consequence) on total economy wide productivity. It turns out that with respect to second moment conditions, the model outperforms not only standard real business cycle (RBC) but also other models with endogenous firm entry (in particular the one of Bilbiie et al. (2012)). Regarding the role of monetary policy, it can be shown that the central bank has an impact on the mentioned channel through its influence on firms' cost structure and the entry costs. The postulated transmission mechanism can have an impact notably on the optimal policy pursued by the central bank.

The empirical part is finally provided in the fourth chapter. Based on a large panel with 345,963 observations of quarterly firm and product price data of non-tradable services, underlying the Swiss sectoral CPIs from 1993 to 2012, we examine how firms set and adjust their prices depending on macroeconomic, sectoral and individual conditions. The dataset has two advantages. First, it allows a detailed traceability of the pricing decisions of the identified firms over time (without regular interruption of the price series as is the case for the US CPI). Second, the data set contains information on the size of price changes and not only on its frequency, allowing for a study of price setting behavior at the intensive margin. Singling out one policy measure, it is shown that an increase in the value-added tax (VAT) is over-proportionally reflected in prices, although the costs of the concerned producers increase only proportionally due to the deductibility of input cost. In addition to that, an increase in the VAT also leads to a decrease in the variance of prices. Furthermore, the results show for the sectors in our sample (non-tradable services) that an appreciation of the Swiss franc leads to an increase in the probability of a positive price change as well as, although to a less extent, in the average size of price changes. In line with previous research, we find that time-dependent variables are of less importance, with the exemption of seasonality components, i.e., we can observe not only more but also stronger price adjustments in the first quarter of a year. On the other hand, state dependent factors are of clear importance. The probability and also the size of a price change particularly increases the farther away a price is from the average price of this product in the sample. All these findings can be of particular interest for monetary policy regarding inflation forecast and also with respect to the impact of central banks' policy measures.

2 Can Monetary Policy Delay the Reallocation of Capital?*

Abstract

This chapter examines the medium-run effects of monetary policy and focuses its analyses on the consequences of distorted (in the sense of exogenously influenced) real interest rates that are currently observed in many industrialized countries. In our model, real interest rates that are too low hinder economic recovery because such rates allow relatively unproductive firms to remain in the market. Monetary policy should increase interest rates after a negative macroeconomic shock to force a reallocation of production factors to more productive firms. We show that there is a trade-off between the short-run and medium-run preferences of the central bank as a consequence. From a welfare perspective, the impact of monetary policy depends on the long-run interest rate relative to the welfare-maximizing interest rate because of the preference for variety in the model.

Keywords: Monetary Policy Design, Reallocation of Capital, Structural Change, Heterogeneous Firms

JEL-Classification: E32, E43, E50, E52

*I thank Reto Föllmi, Johannes Fritz, Jürg Müller, Frédéric Pittet, Rafael Plessow, Lukas Schmid, Darius Stuker, and the participants of the 2012 congress of the Swiss Society of Economics and Statistics in Zurich, the May 24, 2012, Sinergia-Seminar at the University of Zurich, and the 2013 "Structural Change, Dynamics, and Economics Growth" conference in Livorno for helpful comments. All remaining errors are mine.

2.1 Introduction

After the recent financial crisis, monetary authorities around the world resolutely intervened and have thus far prevented the world economy from suffering through a second Great Depression (as was experienced in the 1930s). Nevertheless, it is sobering that the US, the countries in the Euro area, and other industrialized economies are in their seventh year of less-than-potential growth (as indicated by the output gap according to measures of the International Monetary Fund (IMF)).[2] A quick turnaround is not in sight. Central banks have reacted to these ongoing recessional tendencies with more monetary *stimuli* as part of an unconventional monetary policy (i.e., "quantitative easing"). Data on interest rates show that at least the US Federal Reserve (FED) has been successful with its policy regarding its impact on interest rates. Figure 2.1 depicts the development of real interest rates for several maturities (illustrated by inflation-protected T-Bills) in the US between 2003 and 2014, which reveals a continuous and sustainable decrease in the real interest rate for all maturities considered.[3] Thus, central banks seem to be able to influence real interest rates to the extent that they are not lower for real, structural reasons.

---

[2] cp. IMF (2014).

[3] This impression is supported by empirical evidence. In a regression of the real interest rates on their lags, a constant, and the official federal funds rate, a Quandt-Andrews test indicates that there is a structural break in the constant for the entire sample, whereas it does not demonstrate a similar finding for a time-restricted pre-crisis sample (the latter result is consistent with Gerlach and Moretti (2011)). This implies a statistically significant decrease in real interest rates for 5- and 7-year maturities. No significant result can be depicted for the other 20- and 10-year maturities. See appendix 2.A for the detailed results of the econometric analysis.

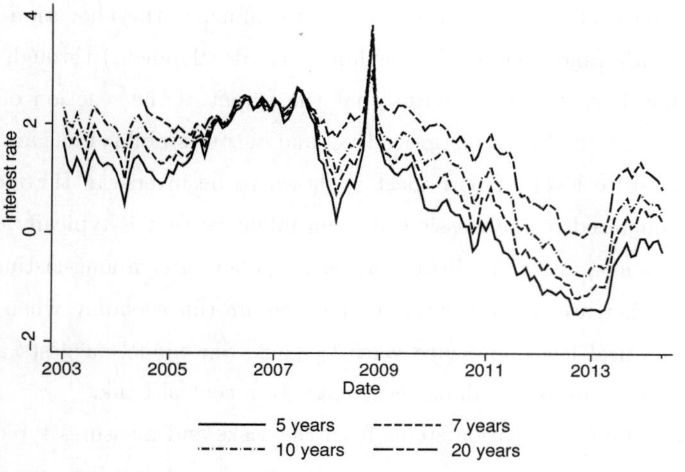

Figure 2.1: US monthly real interest rates (inflation-protected T-Bills).
Data are available for the 2003M01-2014M05 period, and for 20-, 10-, 7-, and 5-year maturities.
Data on 20-year maturities from 2004M07 onwards. *Source:* US Department of the Treasury.

This chapter analyses the potential effects of "distorted" real interest rates in a simple industrial model with heterogeneous firms, as developed by Hopenhayn (1992) and advanced by Melitz (2003). Both models assume heterogeneous productivity. Whereas Melitz (2003) focuses on the implications of trade on the structure of an economy, we consider the influence of monetary policy on the allocation of capital in an economy through its impact on firms' cost structures. We mainly contribute to the literature by proving existence and uniqueness of an equilibrium where increasing interest rates make the cost of borrowing too expensive for relatively unproductive firms, which forces them to exit the market. Thus, the resources of these firms can be reallocated to more productive use. Higher interest rates therefore increase average productivity and quantitative output but reduce variety. Taking into account households' preference for variety, which is given in our model, this implies that there is a welfare-maximizing interest rate.

We assume that central banks are able to influence the allocation of capital in the economy (and therefore its medium-term development) through monetary policy. Indeed, the model suggests that the extent of the reaction of a central bank to fluctuations (regarding price level and output stability) has an impact on output and price level. This impact is shown to be inverse in the medium-run economy compared to the classic short-run influence that is typically considered for central banks, i.e., a stabilizing monetary policy after a long-lasting negative shock must increase interest rates in the medium-run economy when output is below its natural level, and vice versa.[4] Thus, our model suggests a trade-off between short-term and medium-term goals for a central bank.

This important observation stems from the tasks and measures typically faced by central banks in nearly all industrialized countries: stabilizing consumer prices and dampening the effects of business cycles, particularly of recessions.[5] To fulfill these goals, it is common wisdom that interest rates are lowered in a recession, stimulating investment and helping economic development to recover. Conversely, when fighting inflation and stabilizing prices, central banks reduce the money supply, which implies increasing interest rates. Nevertheless, this situation might only hold for the short-run because of the abovementioned trade-off. However, it appears that central banks do not consider this potential conflict and its impact on capital allocation. During long-lasting recessions, ignoring this conflict may delay economic recovery to a certain extent and may derogate future growth possibilities because productive firms cannot actualize their full potential.

Our work relates to the literature that addresses the fact that we currently observe neither an economic recovery nor extraordinary inflation despite low interest rates in many industrialized countries. Some authors argue that this is because

[4]Note that Schmitt-Grohé and Uribe (2012) also postulate a policy of increasing interest rates in their model with a liquidity trap to escape a jobless recovery.

[5]There is an ongoing discussion in the literature on whether central banks should also consider other goals, such as fighting asset price bubbles or stabilizing the financial system; see, e.g., Bernanke and Gertler (2001).

we are in a liquidity trap (e.g., Schmitt-Grohé and Uribe (2012); Werning (2011); Mertens and Ravn (2011)).[6] Others require certain additional assumptions, such as credit constraints (e.g., Guerrieri and Lorenzoni (2011) or Hall (2011)). Whereas these papers continue to use a short-run perspective, we provide an explanation for the phenomenon of an economy that no longer reacts to monetary *stimuli* from a medium-run perspective (i.e., flexible prices but sluggish capital stock or input shares used), as postulated by Solow (2000) or Blanchard (1997).

The rest of the chapter is organized as follows. Section 2.2 provides an overview of the existing literature on the conventionally proposed medium- and long-run impacts of monetary policy. In section 2.3, the components of the new model proposed in this chapter are developed, and section 2.4 describes how the long-run steady state is determined. Section 2.5 incorporates the central bank as a policy maker. For demonstrative purposes, a simulation is performed in section 2.6 to show the consequences of different monetary policies. Section 2.7 finally concludes.

2.2 Review of related literature

Monetary policy generally finds its place only in research on business cycles in which new Keynesian models have been the primary workhorse for many years. This is a logical consequence of the generally accepted neutrality of monetary policy in the long-run economy. Authors who address the medium- or long-run impacts of monetary policy typically propose an indirect analysis by focusing on the potential consequences of the stabilizing effect of monetary policy.

Given the stabilizing effect of monetary policy, the relevant question now concerns the general relationship between business cycles and growth. The intellectual father of this idea is Joseph Schumpeter (1939), who formulated this concept as the "theory of creative destruction" in the 1930s. He stipulates that recessions are necessary to establish new technologies and production processes that will increase

[6] There are similar papers for the case of Japan; see, e.g., Krugman (1998).

the long-run output of the economy. Whereas Schumpeter (1939) provides only a qualitative description, Aghion and Howitt (1992) bring the idea into a tractable model. The driving force of this model is the prospect of potential monopoly profits from new innovations that crowd out old inventions (representing the literal process of "creative destruction"). A similar mechanism is used in an earlier work by Aghion and Saint-Paul (1991).

Other authors have supported this view on the positive effects of recessions and therefore provide, at least implicitly, a critical view of the stabilizing policies of monetary authorities. Notably, the theoretical motivations differ substantially. Caballero and Hammour (1994) argue that creation or innovation is a costly process that is optimally smoothed over time. On the contrary, destruction is a cost-free process. Consequently, recessions (simply modeled as exogenous demand shocks) have a cleansing effect on the economy. Outdated units are destroyed, and there is simultaneously a relatively high rate of innovation. Essential to the outcome of the predictions by this model is the cost function of creation, which is treated as an exogenously given black box. Mortensen and Pissarides (1994) find similar results in the context of a search model that focuses on unemployment.

Conversely, there is also a wide body of literature that postulates a negative relationship between economic fluctuations and long-term growth. The theoretical reasoning for this branch of the literature resides in the effects of so-called "learning by doing", which has been first proposed by Arrow (1962). A more recent model based on this idea is developed by Martin and Rogers (1997). Its rationale may be described as the positive external effect of production on future productivity. Given that this effect decreases with increasing production, there is a negative relationship between business-cycle volatility and productivity in the economy. Blackburn (1999) represents an essential contribution to the literature because he incorporated the "learning-by-doing" effect in a model with "creative destruction"; he merges the two models, which results in the finding that stabilization policy has a negative impact on growth capability.

Empirical results reveal an unclear picture and do not support either view. Galí and Hammour (1993), Saint-Paul (1993), and, more recently, Broda and Weinstein (2007) favor Schumpeter's hypothesis. The contrary position is mainly represented by Ramey and Ramey (1995), who find clear evidence of a negative relationship between volatility and growth in a sample of more than 95 countries. Martin and Rogers (2000) find a similar result when focusing on the cyclicality of unemployment. Although the empirical results are not conclusive, there is a tendency for micro-data, in particular, to support the "creative destruction" view (also postulated by Caballero and Hammour (1994)).

Due to developments following the financial crisis, more recent work focuses on the potential stabilizing impact of monetary policy in conjunction with the consequences of low interest rate policies and/or unconventional monetary policy instruments.[7] Aghion et al. (2012) provide an empirical investigation that demonstrates that pro-cyclical real interest rates in interaction with credit constraints have a positive effect on labor productivity. Chu and Cozzi (2014) introduce a cash-in-advance constraint in a Schumpeterian R&D model. Due to the possibility of encouraging overinvestment in R&D, a policy of low interest rates may be welfare decreasing. Contrary to the previous literature, we consider the medium-term effects of low interest rates by focusing on the survival rate of firms. Nevertheless, the proposed impact of monetary policy is related to the "creative destruction" hypothesis in a broader sense.

2.3 The model

The model presented here draws on Melitz (2003) and incorporates heterogeneous firms in the same style. The model is assumed to describe medium-run development in an economy as proposed by Solow (2000) or Blanchard (1997). As

[7] Some earlier studies did this implicitly by analyzing the welfare consequences of the Friedman rule. See Bhattacharya et al. (2005) for an overview and a recent example.

related to the model, a fixed capital stock is assumed that cannot be decreased or increased in reaction to changing real interest rates that are determined by the central bank.[8] Houses or machines cannot simply be liquidized or enhanced to a great extent, as it is frequently modeled in macroeconomic research. In fact, these are time-consuming processes.

The model consists of a two-sector economy with monopolistic competition. Unanticipated shocks are the source of economic fluctuations and therefore are the justification for an active monetary policy. The model is static.

2.3.1 Households

It is assumed that the economy consists of a constant population of identical households normalized to one. These households own the total capital stock (denoted by $\overline{K}$) and all technologies in the economy. The preferences of a representative household are given by a Stone-Geary-style utility function over a continuum of goods indexed by ω,[9]

$$U = \int_{\omega \in \Omega} \left[ln(c(\omega) + q) - ln(q) \right] d\omega, \tag{2.1}$$

where $c(\omega)$ describes consumption of a specific variety, and q is a common preference parameter. The budget constraint reads as $\int_{\omega \in \Omega} p(\omega)c(\omega)d\omega \leqslant I$, where I denotes the income of a household. Total consumption is the integral over the consumption of all consumed varieties and denoted as C. It is assumed that M varieties are produced in the economy. Households maximize their utility, which

[8]This is generally a well-established approach and is used in older monetary models, in particular. See, for example, Barro and Gordon (1983) or Rogoff (1985).

[9]The Stone-Geary-style utility function is chosen because it allows for a more generalized form (i.e., variable elasticity of substitution) than the standard constant elasticity of substitution (CES) utility function, which is used by Melitz (2003), for example. Kongsamut et al. (2001) describe it as a short way to "embed different income elasticities in a parsimonious way" (p. 875). They also claim that this type of utility specification is supported empirically.

results in the following demand function for a specific variety, ω:

$$c(\omega) = p(\omega)^{1}\left[\frac{I}{M} + q\overline{p}\right] - q, \tag{2.2}$$

where $\overline{p} \equiv \frac{1}{M}\int_{\omega\in\Omega} p(\omega)d\omega$ is the average price of the consumed goods. Demand increases with average price, which can be interpreted as the relative price of the other goods, and higher income, and it decreases with higher price and greater product variety. These are standard properties in models with differentiated goods.

2.3.2 Production

Each firm produces a different variety, ω. Capital must be borrowed from households at a common (net) interest rate, r. Production occurs by a linear constant-return-to-scale production function. All firms face identical fixed costs, $f > 0$, but different marginal costs or, more precisely, different productivity levels that are denoted by $\varphi > 0$. Firms draw their initial productivity, φ, from a common continuous probability distribution, $g(\varphi)$, which is defined over the interval $[0, \infty)$. The continuous cumulative distribution is $G(\varphi)$. Individual production is given by $y(\varphi) = \varphi(k(\varphi) - f)$. Thus, the pricing rule for every firm is

$$p(\varphi) = \sqrt{\frac{r}{\varphi q}\left[\frac{I}{M} + q\overline{p}\right]}, \tag{2.3}$$

based on its profit maximization considerations and depending on its individual productivity, φ. Given this pricing rule, the profit function of an individual firm reads as

$$\pi(\varphi) = \left(\sqrt{\frac{I}{M} + q\overline{p}} - \sqrt{\frac{rq}{\varphi}}\right)^2 - rf. \tag{2.4}$$

This can be interpreted as the profit from regular production minus payment for fixed costs. Note that payment for fixed costs depends on the interest rate or, more technically, on the common marginal cost factor, which is how the interest rate can be interpreted. This is because fixed costs are paid in units of capital whose price varies with the interest rate.

2.3.3 Zero cut-off profit condition

To make profits, a firm must reach a minimum productivity level, φ^* (cut-off productivity). Otherwise, the firm would drop out of the market. The price that a firm facing this cut-off productivity level charges is normalized to one ($p(\varphi^*) = 1$), i.e., this firm produces the numéraire. The cut-off productivity level is calculated by setting the profit function equal to zero and solving for φ. Thus, we have

$$\varphi^* = \frac{r}{1 - \frac{rf}{\frac{I}{M} + q(\overline{p}\quad 1)}} = \frac{rc(\varphi^*)}{c(\varphi^*) - rf}. \tag{2.5}$$

It follows that $\frac{\partial \varphi^*}{\partial r} > 0 \; \forall \; r > 0$.[10] This result is economically intuitive because it simply posits that the cut-off firm must reach a higher level of productivity with increasing costs of borrowing capital to stay in the market. The most important consequence of this process is that some capital resources become available after an increase of the interest rate, r, that can be reallocated to other firms that are more productive. Furthermore, for every producer that drops out of the market, unproductive fixed costs can be avoided. Unfortunately, one would also have to accept a reduced number of varieties because production is more expensive.

2.3.4 Aggregation

As previously discussed, an equilibrium is characterized by a mass, M, of firms (and therefore varieties). This mass is based on a finite total number of potential goods, $\omega \in \Omega$, which is defined as M_0. The term "firm" should be interpreted in a broad sense in our context, it could also refer to particular technologies or sectors. It is self-evident to assume the existing technologies - and therefore the potential varieties - as given in a static medium-run model because developing new technologies is a time-consuming and dynamic process.[11] Because a fraction

[10] Formal proof is part of appendix 2.B.1.

[11] Note that Dixit and Stiglitz (1977) implicitly use the same approach.

$G(\varphi^*)$ of all firms does not produce, the mass of varieties is given by[12]

$$M = M_0(1 - G(\varphi^*)). \tag{2.6}$$

Given the share of non-producing firms, $G(\varphi^*)$, the distribution of producing firms is conditional on $[\varphi^*, \infty)$. Thus, the average price, $\overline{p}$, is given by

$$\overline{p} = \frac{1}{M} \int_{\varphi^*}^{\infty} p(\varphi) M \frac{g(\varphi)}{1 - G(\varphi^*)} d\varphi. \tag{2.7}$$

Inserting the pricing equation (2.3), we implicitly obtain the productivity of a firm charging $\overline{p}$:

$$\tilde{\varphi}(\varphi^*) := \left(\frac{1}{1 - G(\varphi^*)} \int_{\varphi^*}^{\infty} \frac{1}{\sqrt{\varphi}} g(\varphi) d\varphi \right)^2. \tag{2.8}$$

Note that $\tilde{\varphi}$ is an important reference for the productivity of the economy. However, contrary to Melitz (2003), there is no possible direct link to total production in the economy. This is because $\tilde{\varphi}$ is a pure average productivity measure (not a weighted measure).

Solving the quadratic equation (2.7) for $\overline{p}$ gives us the average price charged in this economy:

$$\overline{p} = \frac{1}{2} \sqrt{\frac{r}{\tilde{\varphi}}} \left(\sqrt{\frac{r}{\tilde{\varphi}}} \pm \sqrt{\frac{r}{\tilde{\varphi}} + \frac{4I}{Mq}} \right). \tag{2.9}$$

Because prices cannot be negative, this equation may only have a positive solution. The average price level, $\overline{p}$, rises with a higher interest rate, which indicates that production costs are shifted to consumers. Furthermore, $\overline{p}$ increases as household income rises but decreases with a higher number of producing firms, i.e., with stronger competition. In what follows, this average price is treated as a measure for the general price level; that is, it works as a proxy for a price index.[13]

[12] One could also interpret this as the fraction $G(\varphi^*)$ of all known technologies is not in use.
[13] The same strategy is used by Melitz and Ottaviano (2008).

Because the entire production is consumed, we can sum up over the continuum of all producing firms by using the demand function (2.2) and the pricing rule (2.3), obtaining total output, Y:

$$Y = M\left(\sqrt{\frac{q}{r}\left[\frac{I}{M} + q\overline{p}\right]} \int_{\varphi^*}^{\infty} \sqrt{\varphi}\frac{g(\varphi)}{1-G(\varphi^*)}d\varphi - q\right). \tag{2.10}$$

Note that $\frac{\partial Y}{\partial r} > 0 \; \forall \; r > 0$, but $\frac{\partial Y}{\partial f} < 0$. The first result is not surprising because it is a central feature of the model that a higher interest rate encourages the reallocation of capital from less to more productive firms.[14] However, the latter result is not as obvious. It should be borne in mind that higher fixed costs always affect the entire economy, not only relatively unproductive firms (which are, however, most likely to exit after a rise in fixed costs). That is, potential newly available capital to relatively productive firms is more than completely depleted by higher fixed costs.

The last missing piece to close the model is household income. Households receive an interest rate payment for lending their capital and, because they are their owners, all the profits that firms make. Note that lending to firms is the only way that households can use their capital; the entire capital stock, $\overline{K}$, is therefore always used in production. Utilizing the individual profit function (2.4), this means that

$$I = r\overline{K} + \int_{\varphi^*}^{\infty} M\pi(\varphi)\frac{g(\varphi)}{1-G(\varphi^*)}d\varphi = r\overline{K} + M\left(\frac{I}{M} - \overline{p}q + rq\overline{\varphi} - rf\right), \tag{2.11}$$

where $\overline{\varphi} \equiv \int_{\varphi^*}^{\infty} \frac{1}{\varphi}\frac{g(\varphi)}{1 \; G(\varphi^*)}d\varphi$.

Using the definition (2.9) for $\overline{p}$, we obtain

$$I = r\frac{(\overline{K} + M(q\overline{\varphi} - f))^2\tilde{\varphi} - (\overline{K} + M(q\overline{\varphi} - f))Mq}{Mq^2}. \tag{2.12}$$

Equation (2.12) implies a direct one-to-one effect of the interest rate, r, on household income as a consequence of the income of capital lending. However,

[14] A formal proof is included as part of appendix 2.B.3.

a change in r also affects the cut-off productivity, φ^*. This has two effects. On the one hand, the measure for the average productivity, $\tilde{\varphi}$, becomes higher, which leads to an increase in production and profits per firm; on the other hand, the number of firms decreases, and fewer firms can pay their profits to households. The first effect dominates. This is economically intuitive because total production is strictly increasing in r, i.e., the potential profit base increases.[15]

Because the definition for household income closes the model, the following proposition can be made.

Proposition 1. *For any given set of parameters* $[r > 0, f > 0, q > 0, \overline{K} > 0, M_0 > 0]$ *and distribution* $G(\varphi)$ *defined over the interval* $[0, \infty)$*, the economy is characterized by a unique and stationary equilibrium.*

Proof. See appendix 2.B.1.

Contrary to Melitz (2003), in equilibrium, the firm-level determinants (φ^*, $\tilde{\varphi}$, $\overline{p}$) are not independent of the size of the economy, which can be approximated by $\overline{K}$. A higher capital stock enables more firms to stay in the market. This is a consequence of different preferences and the exogenously fixed maximum number of varieties, M_0. For the interpretation of the equilibrium at this point, consider the interest rate, r, and the capital stock, $\overline{K}$, as exogenously given. Section 2.4 provides an illustration of their formation.

2.3.5 Welfare analysis

Welfare is determined by two factors in this economy, as it is in most models with monopolistic competition. First, individual utility increases with the number of consumed units of each product, whereas the marginal return of each additional unit consumed is diminishing. Second, consumers are variety lovers; they enjoy a

[15] Formal proof is included as part of appendix 2.B.1.

wider range of differentiated products from which they can select. Given a specific equilibrium, welfare is given by the utility of the representative household,

$$U = \frac{M_0}{2}\left[\int_{\varphi^*}^{\infty} ln(\varphi)g(\varphi)d\varphi + (1 - G(\varphi^*))ln\left(\frac{I}{rqM} + \frac{\overline{p}}{r}\right)\right]. \tag{2.13}$$

An increase in r leads to an amplification of production as well as a reduction in the number of producing firms. Welfare, however, depends on both dimensions, which leads to the following proposition.

Proposition 2. $\exists$ *a welfare-maximizing interest rate* $\mathfrak{r} \in [0, \infty)$.

Proof. See appendix 2.B.2.

This indicates that there is an interest rate that ensures the optimal combination of production volume and variety. This result is consistent with the general trade-off of quantity versus diversity in monopolistic competition models, which is described by Dixit and Stiglitz (1977), who also propose that there is an optimal allocation of existing resources. As opposed to their approach of influencing the allocation by constraining the number of firms, this effect can result from adjusting the interest rate in our model.

2.4 The long-run steady state

Thus far, the interest rate, r, and the capital stock, $\overline{K}$, have been treated as free parameters without economic substantiation. This is now changed, and we now put the model in a dynamic Ramsey-Cass-Koopmans (RCK) framework, which enables us to investigate how the capital stock is accumulated and how the long-run interest rate is determined.[16] Individuals face the following long-run dynamic

[16]cp. Ramsey (1928), Cass (1965), and Koopmans (1965).

optimality condition:

$$\max_{C(t),K(t)} \int_0^{\infty} \left[e^{-\rho t} U(C(t)) + \mu(t) \underbrace{(I(t) - C(t))}_{=\dot{K}(t)} \right] dt, \tag{2.14}$$

where t is the time index, ρ is the time preference of individuals, $\mu(t)$ is the Lagrange multiplier, and $U(C(t))$ is the utility from total consumption in one period, t.[17] Because we are only interested in the steady state, we focus on the corresponding asset-pricing equation.[18] Individuals do not take into account the impact of their capital accumulation on the profits generated by firms but only on the return of capital, r.[19] This yields the following optimization rule:

$$\dot{\mu}(t) = \rho\mu(t) - \frac{\partial[r(t)K(t)]}{\partial K(t)}\mu(t). \tag{2.15}$$

In a steady state, growth rates are zero, i.e., $\dot{\mu}(t) = 0$.[20] Solving for r yields the steady state interest rate, denoted as r^* (the time index is dropped in what follows because we are in a steady state). Formally, this is $r^* = \rho$, which is the standard result in RCK models and simply indicates that individuals save until the return of additional savings equals their time preference rate.

The (fixed) steady state capital stock can finally be determined from the fact that the entire production must be consumed in the steady state (note that this is also the case in the baseline model from section 2.3). From the production function, we know that the capital used by a single firm is given by $k(\varphi) = \frac{c(\varphi)}{\varphi} + f$. Integrating over all firms gives us the capital stock for the entire economy:

$$\overline{K} = \int_{\varphi^*}^{\infty} Mk(\varphi)\frac{g(\varphi)}{1 - G(\varphi^*)}d\varphi = M\left(\sqrt{\frac{q}{\rho\tilde{\varphi}}\left[\frac{I}{M} + q\overline{p}\right]} - q\overline{\varphi} + f\right). \tag{2.16}$$

[17] i.e., $U(C(t)) = \int_{\omega\in\Omega} [ln(c(\omega, t) + q) - ln(q)]\, d\omega$.

[18] Note that the initial capital stock is assumed to be given and equals $K_0 > 0$.

[19] The "social planner", on the contrary, would do exactly that. His optimization problem and solution is presented in appendix 2.C.

[20] It is assumed that the usual transversality conditions apply.

This closes the steady state version of the model (all other equations from section 2.3 continue to apply, i.e., all other variables are defined by the respective definitions) and determines the values for r^* and $\overline{K}$ for a given set of parameters. It is important to note that the long-run interest rate, r^*, does not equal the welfare-maximizing interest rate, $\mathfrak{r}$.

2.5 The central bank

This section examines the potential impact of monetary policy on our stylized economy. It is assumed that monetary policy is implemented by a non-discretionary central bank, which uses the interest rate as its objective function. As it is standard, the central bank aims for price and output stability.[21]

To capture our basic idea, we assume that the central bank is able to distort the real interest rate. We model this concept as follows: the central bank enforces its policy by imposing a tax (subsidy), τ, on the interest rate paid by firms.[22] Tax revenues (subsidy expenses) are redistributed to (taken from) households. Therefore, interest payment for firms is now given by

$$rk(\varphi) = \hat{r}(1 + \tau)k(\varphi), \tag{2.17}$$

where $\hat{r}$ is the market interest rate. Given the capital stock, $\overline{K}$, the tax generates a revenue of $\tau\hat{r}\overline{K} \equiv T$ (in case of a subsidy, the amount must be taken from the households in the form of a lump-sum tax).[23] Household income therefore becomes

[21]Note that price stability in a narrow sense does not affect welfare. However, central bank policy (which includes the central bank's reaction to changes in the price level) does have an impact on welfare.

[22]Imposing a tax is normally a fiscal act. However, we consider the process a monetary projection for two reasons. First, it is assumed that the policy follows a strict rule, as is normally assumed only for central banks. Second, monetary policy is sometimes assumed to have fiscal effects, such as in Darby (1975).

[23]Note that this only holds for the medium-run economy with a constant capital stock. In the

$$
\begin{aligned}
I &= \hat{r}\overline{K} + \int_{\varphi^*}^{\infty} M\pi(\varphi)\frac{g(\varphi)}{1-G(\varphi^*)}d\varphi + T \\
&= r\overline{K} + \int_{\varphi^*}^{\infty} M\pi(\varphi)\frac{g(\varphi)}{1-G(\varphi^*)}d\varphi. \qquad (2.18)
\end{aligned}
$$

This equals the definition for household income from equation (2.11), which implies that the properties from our model above, in which no explicitly defined interest rate has been used, hold. By setting the tax according to the rule $\tau = \frac{r-\hat{r}}{\hat{r}}$, the central bank is able to implement every feasible interest rate, r.

Proposition 3. *By imposing tax rate $\tau \in [-1, \infty)$ on the interest rate paid by firms whose revenues (or expenses) are redistributed to (or taken from) households, the central bank can implement any interest rate, r, that it desires.*

Proof. Proven in text.

Thus, in what follows, we treat the interest rate as freely settable by the central bank and relinquish an explicit formulation of the tax rate. This approach improves readability without loss of generality.

The central bank is supposed to react to real, non-permanent shocks on the economy. These might be preference shocks, cost shocks, or supply-side shocks to the productivity distribution. Monetary policy reacts to these disturbances by strictly following a simple Taylor-style rule, given by

$$
r = r^* \left(\frac{\overline{p}}{\overline{p}^*}\right)^{\psi} \left(\frac{Y}{Y^*}\right)^{\gamma}. \qquad (2.19)
$$

$\overline{p}^*$ and Y^* denote the average price and the output level in the absence of any shocks (i.e., in the long-run steady state), respectively. ψ and γ are weighting

long-run economy, the capital stock would adjust when a tax is imposed on the interest rate, as in the standard RCK model. See, e.g., Barro (1990) for a discussion.

parameters that describe the reaction of monetary policy to deviations from the long-run steady state. In a standard monetary framework, the signs of ψ and γ would be positive, i.e., the central bank would raise interest rates when the price level and output are above the steady state levels and would decrease them if they are below the steady state levels after the shock.

In this model, however, such a reaction would accelerate the deviation because output and price level are positively correlated with the interest rate. The first observation has been previously explained and is caused by a higher interest rate leading to a reallocation of capital to more productive firms. The second observation is caused by the interest rate working as a common marginal cost factor. An increase would be shifted to consumer prices. A new configuration of monetary policy design is therefore necessary.

Proposition 4. *A stabilizing monetary policy requires $\psi, \gamma < 0$, which implies an inverse Taylor rule for monetary policy.*

Proof. See appendix 2.B.3.

This observation implies a trade-off in the stabilization goal of the central bank between the short-run and the medium-run economies. After a negative demand shock, for example, low interest rates might work to stabilize in the short-run economy. However, in a case with a long-lasting shock, lax monetary policy will most likely delay the reallocation of capital in the medium-run economy by tiering resources at unproductive firms. This lowers production capacity within the economy. Moreover, the monetary authority would possibly prolong economic downturn relative to non-intervention by maintaining a low interest rate.

It is important to note that the welfare aspect of a stabilizing monetary policy is ambiguous. Given that $r^* > \mathfrak{r}$ (i.e., the steady state interest lies above the welfare-maximizing interest), stabilization after a negative shock might not be a desirable policy because of the preference for diversity. This depends on how welfare reacts to a specific shock. Whereas welfare from output volume is always affected in the direction of the shock, the impact on welfare from diversity is arbitrary. This directly implies that stabilization might be welfare improving after a positive shock because it can increase diversity, although stabilization itself has no intrinsic value for the individuals in the model. The following section provides some insights.

2.6 Numerical simulations

The impact of monetary policy on welfare differs depending on the policy parameters ψ and γ in addition to depending on the settlement of the steady state interest rate, r^*, relative to the welfare-maximizing interest rate, $\mathfrak{r}$, after a potential shock. To qualitatively demonstrate these effects, some simulations are performed that show the consequences for welfare under specific monetary policy rules (without any pretensions of a quantitative predication). The model is not analytically solvable due to fundamental non-linearity, i.e., a numerical algorithm is implemented.[24]

It is assumed that productivity is exponentially distributed, i.e., $\varphi \sim \exp(\lambda)$. The exponential distribution is used for two reasons. First, from an economical point of view, $g(\varphi)$ is strictly decreasing in φ, which represents a comprehensible view of reality because relatively productive ideas and technologies are rarer then relatively unproductive ones. Second, this type of distribution is supported over the entire theoretical interval $[0, \infty)$, i.e., it fits the presumptions of the model. This is an advantage relative to the Pareto distribution, which is sometimes used in similar setups.[25]

The chosen parameters allow a differentiation between the two cases discussed above ($r^* < \mathfrak{r}$ and $r* > \mathfrak{r}$). Nevertheless, in both simulations, a demand-side

[24]The algorithm is based on a numerical convergence. The respective code, written in MatLab®, is available upon request.

[25]See, e.g., Melitz and Ottaviano (2008).

preference shock to q is examined. Noting q^* as the steady state value of q, it follows that $q = q^*\varepsilon$, where ε is a positive idiosyncratic shock with mean one. The central bank reacts to the shock by setting the interest rate according to the Taylor rule from equation (2.19). To evaluate the effects of monetary policy, the Taylor rule parameters, ψ and γ, are alternated in the simulation. Although we know from proposition 4 that the stabilization of output and price level requires $\psi, \gamma < 0$, the parameters are allowed to be positive. However, we make the restriction that $\mid \psi \mid < 1$ and $\mid \gamma \mid < 1$, i.e., the marginal reaction of the central bank will not be increasing.

2.6.1 Monetary policy with $r^* < \mathfrak{r}$

We begin with the case in which the steady state interest rate lies below the welfare-maximizing level in the steady state. Regarding parameters, we set λ to 0.5, which allows for a relatively smooth distribution of productivity. The number of potential ideas, M_0, is normalized to one. The preference parameter, q, is also set to one. Fixed costs, f, are set to 20, which simply represents an upscaling for illustrational purposes. The time preference parameter, ρ, is assumed to be 0.04, which implies a realistic long-run interest rate, r^*, of 4%. This combination of parameters implies a steady state capital stock, $\overline{K}$, of 36.68. The welfare-maximizing interest rate, $\mathfrak{r}$, in this case is 0.32 (i.e., 32%), which is far higher than r^* and thus implies that the case with $r^* < \mathfrak{r}$ is the more plausible one. Now, we assume that this model economy is hit by a shock $\varepsilon = 1.05$.

As the model suggests - and consistent with the data - such a demand shock leads to a decline in output and the average price level. The same holds for the number of firms producing and for the utility level, although the effect on the former is very small.[26] Figure 2.2 shows the welfare level relative to the steady state (as a percentage) in dependence on the parameters ψ and γ.

[26]However, this is primarily a consequence of the parameters chosen.

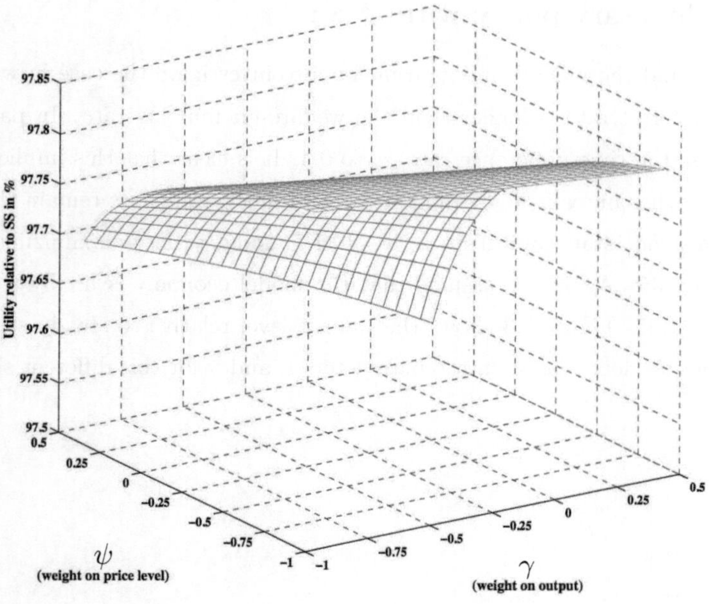

Figure 2.2: Utility after a preference shock depending on monetary policy with $r^* < \mathfrak{r}$.

The figure shows that welfare constantly increases with lower policy parameters; that is, the stabilizing, inverse Taylor rule is also welfare improving after a *negative* shock. This is the case as long as the policy parameters ensure that $r(\psi, \gamma) \leqslant \mathfrak{r}$. This result represents increasing production as a result of the reallocation of capital to relatively more productive firms initialized by the central bank. Note that the effect is non-linear; the marginal impact of a decrease in the policy parameters is diminishing. Individuals rank higher consumption possibilities higher than the loss of variety in this example. As a consequence, there is no conflict between the stabilization goal of the central bank and welfare.

2.6.2 Monetary policy with $r^* > \mathfrak{r}$

To understand the model's mechanism, we also investigate the case in which the long-run interest rate is higher than the welfare-maximizing rate. In particular, we increase the time-preference rate, ρ, to 0.4. It is clear that this implies a very high and rather unrealistic discount rate. All other parameters remain the same, yielding a steady state capital stock, $\overline{K}$, of 34.71 and a welfare-maximizing interest rate, $\mathfrak{r}$, of 0.35. Again, we assume that the model economy is hit by a demand shock $\varepsilon = 1.05$. Figure 2.3 shows the welfare level relative to steady state (as a percentage) in dependence on the parameters ψ and γ for this different situation.

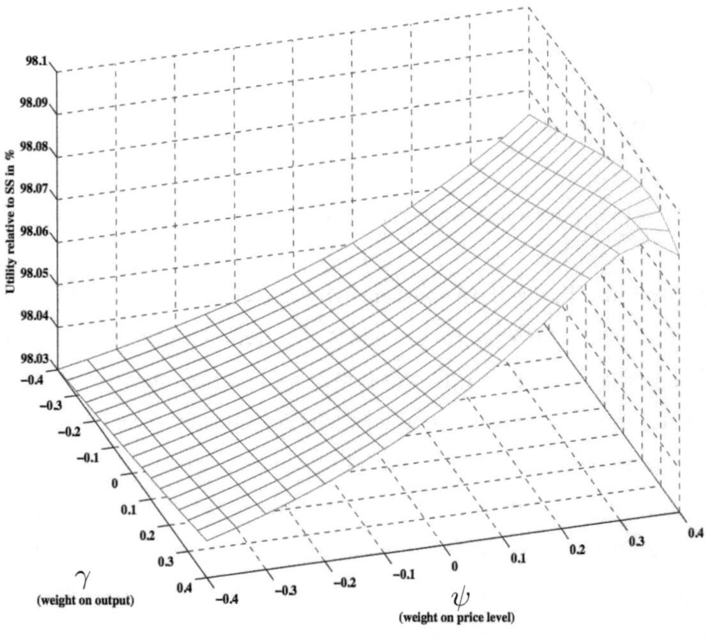

Figure 2.3: Utility after a preference shock depending on monetary policy with $r^* > \mathfrak{r}$.

Contrary to the case described above, welfare-optimizing policy now requires positive values for ψ and γ, although this would shift the economy further away from its steady state. The reason for this is the preference for variety of individuals. From their perspective, monetary policy should permit more firms to enter the market regardless of their relatively low productivity. This example reveals an important insight: stabilizing monetary policy is not always welfare improving in the model. The impact on utility depends on the position of the steady state interest rate relative to the welfare-maximizing interest rate.

Despite this theoretically interesting thought experiment, which must be interpreted in light of the very high time preference rate, we must keep in mind that monetary policy cannot directly influence the structure of the economy in the long-run. This implies that a monetary policy that further amplifies the variance from steady state can never be sustainable. A central bank that wants to stabilize output and the price level in the model should therefore follow the inverse Taylor rule (discussed above) in any case.

2.7 Conclusion

In light of the ongoing and long-lasting period of low interest rates worldwide, we have developed a monopolistic competition model with heterogeneous firms to investigate the impact of monetary policy in the medium-run economy. "Medium run" has been interpreted in the sense that prices are flexible, but the capital stock and the potential amount of variety are assumed to be fixed because adjustments are time consuming. The driving factor is the interest rate through its role as the common marginal cost factor. An increase in the interest rate (induced by the central bank) forces relatively unproductive firms to leave the market because they would make negative profits. We prove existence and uniqueness of an equilibrium where this mechanism allows for capital to be reallocated to relatively more productive firms, which would lead to higher productivity on average and, therefore, to higher output in the economy.

Because of this channel, the model suggests that an output-stabilizing monetary policy should increase interest rates such that the reallocation of capital within the economy in a long-lasting crisis is not delayed. Furthermore, the price level reacts positively to a rising interest rate in the model because of its nature as a common marginal cost factor. This phenomenon may have important implications for monetary authorities because their policy goal is stabilization. Their medium-run Taylor rule becomes inverse, which indicates that they should slow down expansionary monetary policy at some point in a long-lasting crisis. In other words, central banks might face a trade-off in their stabilization goal between the short- and the medium-run. Note that this insight does not imply that monetary authorities should simply induce a sharp switchover of their policy after some time because this would most likely lead to negative short-run distortions. Instead, it suggests a smooth revaluation of monetary policy instruments.

It should be noted that excessive promotion of the reallocation of capital to very productive firms would not be optimal from a welfare perspective. In the context of the model, this is a consequence of the preference for variety. Conversely, the model theoretically suggests that it might be welfare improving, under certain circumstances, to further amplify the deviation from the steady state economy to increase diversity. However, such policies would never be sustainable because the impact of monetary policy diminishes in the long-run economy.

Further research must be conducted regarding the impact of monetary policy on the structural patterns of an economy. A main focus should certainly lie on empirical research investigating, for example, the impact of monetary policy on the structure in particular industries. How do firm entry and exit rates react to a specific interest rate policy when controlling for other factors, and what is the impact on overall productivity? Firm-level data, for example, are a promising source to provide answers to such questions.

Appendix

2.A Structural breaks in the US real interest rates

The test for a structural break in the US real interest rates is based on a regression of the following form:

$$TIPS_{i,t} = \beta_i^1 + \beta_i^2 TIPS_{i,t-1} + \beta_i^3 R_t + \varepsilon_{i,t}, \tag{2.20}$$

where t is a time index, i denotes the maturity, and R is the federal fund rate.[27] It is assumed that a structural break in the constant, β_i^1, indicates a change in the long-term real interest rate. A Quandt-Andrews unknown breakpoint test with 10% trimming is performed for two samples: one for before the crisis (January 2003-January 2007) and one for the entire available sample (January 2003-May 2014). Data on the 20 years maturity are only available from July 2004 onwards. Thus, the corresponding regression is respectively restricted. Table 2.1 summarizes the results.

Test statistics imply a structural break for the longer period but not for the period before the crisis for the 5- and the 7-year maturities (for the 7-year T-Bill; the test statistic is narrowly significant at the 5% significance level for the shorter period). No significant change can be depicted for the 10- and 20-year maturities. Nevertheless, this is an indicator of a monetary policy that is able to influence real interest rates over a long period. It is clear that other explanations, such as changing time preferences, may also play a role.

[27] Monthly data on real interest rates are TIPS data (i.e., inflation-protected treasury bills) from the US Department of the Treasury. Data on the federal fund rate are from the FED.

Table 2.1: Test for a structural break in the US real interest rates.

	Sample	
Maturity	2003M01-2007M01	2003M01-2014M05
5 years	8.78 (2004M08)	13.92** (2008M10)
7 years	9.36* (2004M08)	13.55** (2008M12)
10 years	8.57 (2004M08)	8.47 (2008M12)
20 years	5.93 (2006M03)	8.44 (2011M03)

Notes: Test statistics correspond to the maximum LR F-statistics. ** and * indicate rejection of the null hypothesis of no break point at the 1% and 5% significance levels, respectively. Critical values correspond to Hansen (1997). Suggested break points are in parenthesis.

2.B Proofs

2.B.1 Proof of Proposition 1

Proof. In the following, we show the existence and uniqueness of the equilibrium and the increase of φ^* in r.

Step 1: *Definitions*

For an easier notation, let us define

$$\frac{I}{M} := r \underbrace{\left(\frac{(\overline{K} + M(q\overline{\varphi} - f))^2 \tilde{\varphi} - (\overline{K} + M(q\overline{\varphi} - f))Mq}{(Mq)^2} \right)}_{\equiv B} = rB. \tag{2.21}$$

This implies

$$\overline{p} := \frac{1}{2}\sqrt{\frac{r}{\tilde{\varphi}}}\left(\sqrt{\frac{r}{\tilde{\varphi}}} + \sqrt{\frac{r}{\tilde{\varphi}} + \frac{4rB}{q}}\right) = r\underbrace{\frac{1}{2}\left(\frac{1}{\tilde{\varphi}} + \sqrt{\frac{1}{\tilde{\varphi}^2} + \frac{4B}{q}}\right)}_{\equiv D} = rD. \quad (2.22)$$

The equilibrium of the economy can be described in a single equation by inserting equations (2.12) and (2.9) into the equation for the cut-off productivity (2.5). This yields the following definition:

$$\varphi^* = \frac{r}{1 - \frac{rf}{c(\varphi^*)}} = \frac{r}{1 - \frac{rf}{rB+q(rD-1)}} = \frac{rB + rqD - q}{B + qD - \frac{q}{r} - f} := \mathfrak{f}(r, \varphi^*). \quad (2.23)$$

Given that there is a single φ^* for a given set of parameters $[r > 0, f > 0, q > 0, \overline{K} > 0, M_0 > 0]$ and distribution $G(\varphi)$ defined over the interval $[0, \infty)$, that solves this equation, the economy is characterized by a unique and stationary equilibrium.

Step 2: *Boundary values*

In this step, the boundary values for $\mathfrak{f}(r, \varphi^*)$ are calculated. Note that we have $B > 0$ and, therefore, $D > 0 \; \forall \; \varphi^* \in [0, \infty)$. Furthermore, it holds that $\lim_{\varphi^* \to \infty} B, D = \infty$, implying that

$$\lim_{\varphi^* \to \infty} \mathfrak{f}(r, \varphi^*) = r, \quad (2.24)$$

which is the lowest possible value for φ^*. The same result obtains in the absence of fixed costs. In this case, we would have $\mathfrak{f}(r, \varphi^*) = r \; \forall \; \varphi^*$.

Moreover, we have $\lim_{c(\varphi^*) \to rf} \mathfrak{f}(r, \varphi^*) = \infty$, or, more precisely,

$$\lim_{\varphi^* \to c^{-1}(rf)} \mathfrak{f}(r, \varphi^*) = \infty, \quad (2.25)$$

which is the highest possible value for φ^*. This implies that $\mathfrak{f}(r, \varphi^*)$ is decreasing from ∞ to r as φ^* is increasing from $c^{-1}(rf)$ to ∞.

Step 3: *Derivatives*

If we can show that $\frac{\partial \mathfrak{f}(r,\varphi^*)}{\partial \varphi^*} \leqslant 0 \ \forall \ \varphi^* \in [c\ ^{1}(rf), \infty)$, we have a unique equilibrium (because the left-hand side of equation (2.23) is monotonically increasing).

The derivative of $\mathfrak{f}(r, \varphi^*)$ is given by

$$\frac{\partial \mathfrak{f}(r,\varphi^*)}{\partial \varphi^*} = \frac{-rf\left(r\frac{\partial B}{\partial \varphi^*} + rq\frac{\partial D}{\partial \varphi^*}\right)}{(c(\varphi^*) - rf)^2} = \frac{-f\left(\frac{\partial B}{\partial \varphi^*} + q\frac{\partial D}{\partial \varphi^*}\right)}{(B + qD - \frac{q}{r} - f)^2}. \tag{2.26}$$

This expression is non-positive as long as $r\frac{\partial B}{\partial \varphi^*} + rq\frac{\partial D}{\partial \varphi^*} \geqslant 0$. To show this, let us first provide the derivatives of some variables:

$$\frac{\partial M}{\partial \varphi^*} = -g(\varphi^*)M_0 < 0, \tag{2.27}$$

$$\frac{\partial \overline{\varphi}}{\partial \varphi^*} = \frac{g(\varphi^*)}{1 - G(\varphi^*)}\left[\overline{\varphi} - \frac{1}{\varphi^*}\right] < 0, \tag{2.28}$$

$$\frac{\partial \tilde{\varphi}}{\partial \varphi^*} = 2\tilde{\varphi}^{\frac{2}{3}}\frac{g(\varphi^*)}{1 - G(\varphi^*)}\left[\frac{1}{\sqrt{\varphi^*}} - \tilde{\varphi}\ ^{\frac{1}{2}}\right] > 0. \tag{2.29}$$

These are now used to calculate the derivative of B:

$$\begin{aligned}\frac{\partial B}{\partial \varphi^*} =& \frac{1}{(Mq)^4}[2(\overline{K} + M(q\overline{\varphi} - f))\overbrace{(M_0 g(\varphi^*)(f - \frac{q}{\varphi^*}))}^{\frac{\partial M}{\partial \varphi^*}q\overline{\varphi} + Mq\frac{\partial \overline{\varphi}}{\partial \varphi^*} \quad \frac{\partial M}{\partial \varphi^*}f}\tilde{\varphi}(Mq)^2 + \\ & \frac{\partial \tilde{\varphi}}{\partial \varphi^*}(\overline{K} + M(q\overline{\varphi} - f))^2(Mq)^2 + g(\varphi^*)M_0 q(\overline{K} + M(q\overline{\varphi} - f))(Mq)^2 - \\ & (M_0 g(\varphi^*)(f - \frac{q}{\varphi^*}))(Mq)^3 + \underbrace{2Mg(\varphi^*)M_0 q^2}_{\frac{\partial (Mq)^2}{\partial \varphi^*}}((\overline{K} + M(q\overline{\varphi} - f))^2\tilde{\varphi} \\ & - (\overline{K} + M(q\overline{\varphi} - f))Mq)].\end{aligned} \tag{2.30}$$

It holds that $\frac{\partial B}{\partial \varphi^*} > 0$. This is a consequence of the fact that $\varphi^* \geqslant c\ ^{1}(rf)$. It implies $f - \frac{q}{\varphi^*} \geqslant 0$. Assume $f \geqslant \frac{q}{c\ ^{1}(rf)}$, then it must be that $c\ ^{1}(rf) \geqslant \frac{q}{f} \Leftrightarrow rf \geqslant$

$c(\frac{q}{f})$. This can be observed by inserting $\varphi = \frac{q}{f}$ into the profit function (2.4). It becomes negative, implying that $rf \geqslant c(\frac{q}{f})$.

Furthermore, the derivative of D is given by

$$\begin{aligned}\frac{\partial D}{\partial \varphi^*} &= -\frac{1}{2\tilde{\varphi}^2}\frac{\partial \tilde{\varphi}}{\partial \varphi^*} + \frac{1}{4\sqrt{\frac{1}{\tilde{\varphi}^2}+\frac{4B}{q}}}\left(-2\frac{1}{\tilde{\varphi}^3}\frac{\partial \tilde{\varphi}}{\partial \varphi^*} + \frac{4}{q}\frac{\partial B}{\partial \varphi^*}\right)\\ &= -\frac{1}{2\tilde{\varphi}^3}\frac{\partial \tilde{\varphi}}{\partial \varphi^*}\left(\tilde{\varphi} + \frac{1}{\sqrt{\frac{1}{\tilde{\varphi}^2}+\frac{4B}{q}}}\right) + \frac{\frac{\partial B}{\partial \varphi^*}}{q\sqrt{\frac{1}{\tilde{\varphi}^2}+\frac{4B}{q}}}\\ &= \frac{\frac{\partial B}{\partial \varphi^*}\frac{1}{q}2\tilde{\varphi}^3 - \frac{\partial \tilde{\varphi}}{\partial \varphi^*}\left(1+\tilde{\varphi}\sqrt{\frac{1}{\tilde{\varphi}^2}+\frac{4B}{q}}\right)}{2\tilde{\varphi}^3\sqrt{\frac{1}{\tilde{\varphi}^2}+\frac{4B}{q}}}. \qquad (2.31)\end{aligned}$$

Using (2.30) (the second addend), it can be shown that $\frac{\partial D}{\partial \varphi^*} > 0$. It is a consequence of the fact that

$$\begin{aligned}\frac{\partial \tilde{\varphi}}{\partial \varphi^*}\frac{2\tilde{\varphi}^3\frac{1}{q}(\overline{K}+M(q\overline{\varphi}-f))^2}{(Mq)^2} &> \frac{\partial \tilde{\varphi}}{\partial \varphi^*}\left(1+\tilde{\varphi}\sqrt{\frac{1}{\tilde{\varphi}^2}+\frac{4B}{q}}\right) \Leftrightarrow\\ \frac{\tilde{\varphi}^2(\overline{K}+M(q\overline{\varphi}-f))^2}{(Mq)^2} &> qD \Leftrightarrow\\ r\frac{\tilde{\varphi}^2(\overline{K}+M(q\overline{\varphi}-f))^2}{(Mq)^2} &> q\overline{p}. \qquad (2.32)\end{aligned}$$

From the definition of income (2.12), we know that the left-hand side of the inequality (2.32) is greater than I. Because it cannot be that $I < q\overline{p}$ (otherwise there would be no consumption), the inequality holds. This proves that $\frac{\partial D}{\partial \varphi^*} > 0$.

This finally ensures that $\frac{\partial \mathfrak{f}(r,\varphi^*)}{\partial \varphi^*} > 0$ and therefore proves the existence and uniqueness of the equilibrium.

Note that this result holds as long as $\tilde{\varphi}$, $\overline{\varphi}$ and $\int_{\varphi^*}^{\infty} ln(\varphi)\frac{g(\varphi)}{1-G(\varphi^*)}d\varphi$ are defined. This is normally less restrictive than in Melitz (2003). The reason for this is that we do not have simple CES preferences, which indicates that normally fewer moments must be defined, which allows for more flexibility (depending on the degree of substitutability). In contrast, the Melitz model contains a finitely defined (weighted) average productivity.

Step 4: *Proof of* $\frac{\partial \mathfrak{f}(\varphi^*, r)}{\partial r} > 0$

Finally, we show that $\mathfrak{f}(r, \varphi^*)$, and, therefore, φ^* are increasing in r.

$$\begin{aligned}\frac{\partial \mathfrak{f}(\varphi^*, r)}{\partial r} &= \frac{1}{\left(B + qD - \frac{q}{r} - f\right)^2}[(B + qD)(B + qD - \frac{q}{r} - f) \\ &- \left(\frac{q}{r^2}\right)(rB + rqD - q)] \\ &= (B + qD)(B + qD - \frac{q}{r} - f) - (B + qD)\frac{q}{r} + \left(\frac{q}{r}\right)^2.\end{aligned}$$

This implies that the derivative is positive as long as $(B + qD - \frac{q}{r} - f) \geqslant \frac{q}{r}$. Suppose that this is not the case. Then, we would have

$$\begin{aligned}&\frac{q}{r} \geqslant B + qD - \frac{q}{r} - f \Leftrightarrow \\ &q \geqslant \underbrace{rB + rqD - q}_{=c(\varphi^*)\ \text{(cp. equation 2.2)}} - rf \Leftrightarrow \\ &rf + q \geqslant c(\varphi^*). \qquad (2.33)\end{aligned}$$

However, this contradicts the fact that $\pi(\varphi^*) = c(\varphi^*) - \frac{r}{\varphi^*}c(\varphi^*) - rf = 0$. This implies that φ^* is strictly increasing in r. □

For a better understanding, a graphic analysis of the proof is provided in figure 2.4.

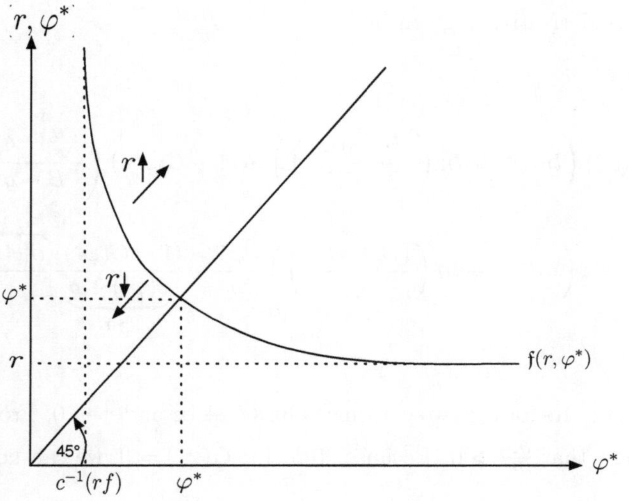

Figure 2.4: Existence and uniqueness of the market equilibrium.

2.B.2 Proof of Proposition 2

Proof. We show that there is a welfare-maximizing interest rate, $\mathfrak{r}$, by demonstrating that the derivative of the utility function can have positive and negative values. Let us first rewrite the welfare function (2.13) as

$$\begin{aligned} U &= \frac{M_0}{2}\left[\int_{\varphi^*}^{\infty} ln(\varphi)g(\varphi)d\varphi + (1 - G(\varphi^*))ln\left(\frac{rB}{rq} + \frac{rD}{r}\right)\right] \\ &= \frac{M_0}{2}\left[\int_{\varphi^*}^{\infty} ln(\varphi)g(\varphi)d\varphi + (1 - G(\varphi^*))ln\left(\frac{B}{q} + D\right)\right]. \end{aligned} \tag{2.34}$$

The respective derivative is given by

$$
\begin{aligned}
\frac{\partial U}{\partial r} &= \frac{\partial U}{\partial \varphi^*}\frac{\partial \varphi^*}{\partial r} \\
&= \frac{M_0}{2}\left[-g(\varphi^*)\left(ln(\varphi^*)+ln\left(\frac{(B+qD)}{q}\right)\right)+(1-G(\varphi^*))\left(\frac{\frac{\partial B}{\partial \varphi^*}+q\frac{\partial D}{\partial \varphi^*}}{B+qD}\right)\right]\frac{\partial \varphi^*}{\partial r} \\
&= \frac{M_0}{2}\left[-g(\varphi^*)\left(ln(\varphi^*)+ln\left(\frac{(B+qD)}{q}\right)\right)\frac{\partial \varphi^*}{\partial r}+\underbrace{\frac{(1-G(\varphi^*))}{c(\varphi^*)+q}}_{\geqslant 0}\frac{\overbrace{\partial[c(\varphi^*)+q]}^{\geqslant 0}}{\partial r}\right].
\end{aligned}
\tag{2.35}
$$

Evaluation occurs for the two extreme values $r \to \infty$ and $r \to 0$. From appendix 2.B.1, we know that $\frac{\partial \varphi^*}{\partial r} > 0$. Because $\lim_{\varphi^* \to \infty} 1 - G(\varphi^*) = 0$, we can note that

$$\lim_{\varphi^*, r \to \infty} \frac{\partial \varphi^*}{\partial r} = -\infty. \tag{2.36}$$

Furthermore because $\frac{(B+qD)}{q}$ is finite, and given that $\lim_{\varphi^* \to 0} ln(\varphi^*) = -\infty$, it follows that

$$\lim_{\varphi^*, r \to 0} \frac{\partial \varphi^*}{\partial r} = \infty. \tag{2.37}$$

This ensures that the derivative of the welfare function with respect to r consists of a positive and a negative part, which proves that there is a welfare-maximizing interest rate, $\mathfrak{r}$. It is clear that more than one interior solution might theoretically exist. However, because computational simulations do not support the relevance of this reservation, it is ignored. □

2.B.3 Proof of Proposition 4

Proof. In the following, we show that a stabilizing Taylor rule must be inverse. This is done by demonstrating that $\frac{d\overline{p}}{dr} > 0 \wedge \frac{dY}{dr} > 0 \; \forall \; r \in [0, \infty)$.

First, the respective derivative for $\overline{p}$ is given by

$$\frac{d\overline{p}}{dr} = \frac{\partial \overline{p}}{\partial r} + \frac{\partial \overline{p}}{\partial \varphi^*}\frac{d\varphi^*}{dr} = D + r\frac{\partial D}{\partial \varphi^*}\frac{d\varphi^*}{dr}. \tag{2.38}$$

From appendix 2.B.1, we know that all parts of this derivate are positive, i.e., $\overline{p}$ is strictly increasing in r.

Second, for the derivative of Y, let us rewrite equation (2.10) for total production as

$$Y = M_0\left(\sqrt{q[B+qD]}\int_{\varphi^*}^{\infty}\sqrt{\varphi}g(\varphi)d\varphi - (1-G(\varphi^*))q\right). \tag{2.39}$$

The interest rate, r, has cancelled out, so we can calculate the respective derivative simply by

$$\frac{\partial Y}{\partial r} = \frac{\partial Y}{\partial \varphi^*}\frac{\partial \varphi^*}{\partial r} = \\ M_0\left(\frac{q\left[\frac{\partial B}{\partial \varphi^*} + q\frac{\partial D}{\partial \varphi^*}\right]}{2\sqrt{q[B+qD]}}\int_{\varphi^*}^{\infty}\sqrt{\varphi}g(\varphi)d\varphi - \sqrt{q[B+qD]}g(\varphi^*)\sqrt{\varphi^*} + g(\varphi^*)q\right)\frac{\partial \varphi^*}{\partial r}. \tag{2.40}$$

This equation is positive as long as

$$0.5\left[\frac{\partial B}{\partial \varphi^*} + q\frac{\partial D}{\partial \varphi^*}\right]\int_{\varphi^*}^{\infty}\sqrt{\varphi}g(\varphi)d\varphi \geqslant (B+qD)g(\varphi^*)\sqrt{\varphi^*}. \tag{2.41}$$

Using equation (2.31), we know that

$$\frac{\partial B}{\partial \varphi^*} + q\frac{\partial D}{\partial \varphi^*} = \frac{\left(1+\sqrt{\frac{1}{\tilde{\varphi}^2}+\frac{4B}{q}}\right)\frac{\partial B}{\partial \varphi^*} - \left(\tilde{\varphi}+\sqrt{\frac{1}{\tilde{\varphi}^2}+\frac{4B}{q}}\right)\frac{q}{2\tilde{\varphi}^3}\frac{\partial \tilde{\varphi}}{\partial \varphi^*}}{\sqrt{\frac{1}{\tilde{\varphi}^2}+\frac{4B}{q}}}. \tag{2.42}$$

Given the derivative of B, equation (2.30), the second addend ensures that this expression is positive, i.e., the other parts of the equation can be used to show that the condition mentioned is fulfilled. This indicates that the inequality condition (2.41) from above can be reduced to

$$\left(\sqrt{\frac{1}{\tilde{\varphi}^2}+\frac{4B}{q}}\right)0.5\overbrace{\left[g(\varphi^*)M_0q(\overline{K}+M(q\overline{\varphi}-f))(Mq)^{\;\;2}+2Mg(\varphi^*)M_0q^2\frac{B}{(Mq)^2}\right]}^{\text{3rd \& 5th addend of eq. (2.30)}}$$

$$\int_{\varphi^*}^{\infty}\sqrt{\varphi}g(\varphi)d\varphi$$

$$\geqslant\left(\sqrt{\frac{1}{\tilde{\varphi}^2}+\frac{4B}{q}}\right)(B+qD)g(\varphi^*)\sqrt{\varphi^*}\Leftrightarrow$$

$$[(\overline{K}+M(q\overline{\varphi}-f))(Mq)^{\;\;1}+B]\int_{\varphi^*}^{\infty}\sqrt{\varphi}\frac{g(\varphi)}{1-G(\varphi^*)}d\varphi\geqslant(B+qD)\sqrt{\varphi^*}\Leftrightarrow$$

$$\left[r(\overline{K}+M(q\overline{\varphi}-f))(Mq)^{\;\;1}+\frac{I}{M}\right]\int_{\varphi^*}^{\infty}\sqrt{\varphi}\frac{g(\varphi)}{1-G(\varphi^*)}d\varphi\geqslant(\frac{I}{M}+q\overline{p})\sqrt{\varphi^*}. \tag{2.43}$$

Given that $r(\overline{K}+M(q\overline{\varphi}-f))(Mq)^{\;\;1}>I$ (from equation (2.12)), it also holds that $r(\overline{K}+M(q\overline{\varphi}-f))(Mq)^{\;\;1}>q\overline{p}$; otherwise, there would be no consumption. Furthermore, it holds that $\int_{\varphi^*}^{\infty}\sqrt{\varphi}\frac{g(\varphi)}{1\ \ G(\varphi^*)}d\varphi>\sqrt{\varphi^*}$. Together, this ensures that the inequality condition holds and that, therefore, Y is strictly increasing in r, which closes the proof. □

2.C Optimization by the social planner

The social planner solves the optimization problem from equation (2.14) and considers the impact of the capital stock on the (positive) profits of the firms. The corresponding asset pricing equation therefore becomes

$$\dot{\mu}(t)=\rho\mu(t)-\frac{\partial I(t)}{\partial K(t)}\mu(t). \tag{2.44}$$

In a steady state, growth rates are zero, i.e., $\dot{\mu}(t)=0$.[28] Using the definition for *total* income from equation (2.12) and solving for r yields the steady state interest

[28]It is again assumed that the usual transversality conditions apply.

rate that a social planer would obtain, denoted by

$$r^*_{social} := \frac{\rho M q^2}{2\tilde{\varphi}(\overline{K} + M(q\overline{\varphi} - f)) - Mq}. \tag{2.45}$$

Following the argumentation from section 2.4, the long-run capital stock determined by the social planner is then given by

$$\overline{K} = M\left(\sqrt{\frac{q}{r^*_{social}\tilde{\varphi}}\left[\frac{I}{M} + q\overline{p}\right]} - q\overline{\varphi} + f\right). \tag{2.46}$$

The optimization of the social planner entails an equilibrium with a lower interest rate and a higher capital stock, as observed in equations (2.45) and (2.46). This result is not surprising because the social planner considers the effect of an additional unit of capital on the profits that individuals receive from the firms, i.e., he internalizes the external effect of capital accumulation on profits. The positive effect of capital on profits implies that it is worth saving more than in the decentralized case, which leads to the effects discussed above. However, the qualitative impact of monetary policy as described in sections 2.5 and 2.6 also holds with a social planner.

3 Business Cycles and Monetary Policy with Productivity Heterogeneity**

Abstract

This chapter describes a new channel of the exogenous technology shock amplification mechanism induced by firm entry and exit. A new Keynesian model with endogenous net business formation and heterogeneous productivity is developed for this purpose. Economic expansion leads to higher entry rates and thus increasing competition, producing two outcomes. First, the cut-off productivity level that a firm must reach to achieve positive profits rises, and thus, average productivity within an economy also increases. Second, higher competition and average productivity lower the cost of market entry, which may amplify the first effect. With respect to second-moment conditions, the model outperforms standard real business cycle as well as other models that include endogenous firm entry. Moreover, monetary policy can influence the aforementioned channels, as it affects firms' production and market entry costs. This new transmission mechanism of monetary policy may also affect the optimal policies pursued by a central bank.

Keywords: Business Cycles, New Keynesian Models, Productivity, Heterogeneous Firms

JEL-Classification: E32, E43, E50, E52

**I am gratefully indebted to Reto Föllmi, Johannes Fritz, Federico Ravenna and Carlo Strub for their helpful comments. Remaining errors are of course my own responsibility.

3.1 Introduction

Relationships and interactions between net business and product formations and business cycles are a topic of increasing debate in the existing literature due to empirical observations that the number of producing firms and degree of product variety are strongly pro-cyclical phenomena. An early empirical investigation of this trend is conducted by Dunne et al. (1988) for the manufacturing sector. Similar findings are presented by Devereux et al. (1996) and, more recently, Jaimovich and Floetotto (2008), who report a strong negative correlation between the number of failing firms and business cycles for both the entire economy and for separate industries. Recent studies by Bernard et al. (2010) and Broda and Weinstein (2010) analyze this issue at the product level. Both studies find that product creation strongly affects GDP growth (approximately 9% of all products in terms of output value are replaced each year) as well as pro-cyclical product creation movement.[29]

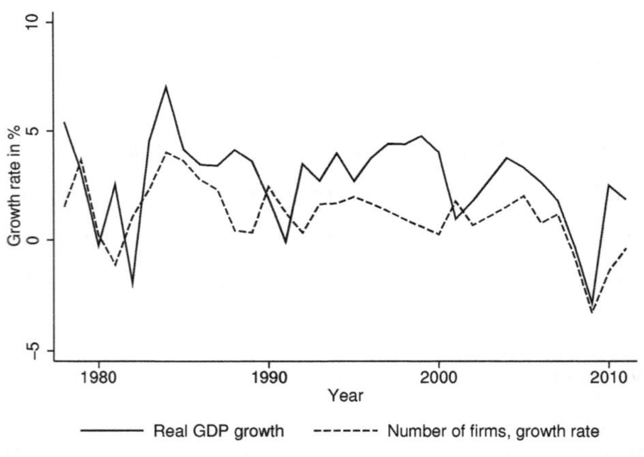

Figure 3.1: Yearly real GDP growth vs. net business formation in the US, 1978-2011.
Source: US Census Bureau and US Bureau of Economic Analysis.

[29]See Bilbiie et al. (2012) for a concise summary of these two papers.

Figure 3.1 illustrates the cyclicality of net business formation in comparison to real GDP growth in the US for the 1978-2011 period (yearly data). The contemporaneous correlation between the two time series is 0.54 and highly significant.

The model developed in this chapter accounts for these empirical observations and provides a mechanism that induces an amplification of exogenous technology shocks through the entry/exit actions of individual firms.[30] More precisely, we study the role of endogenous producer entry and exit through a new Keynesian dynamic stochastic general equilibrium (DSGE) framework that includes firm heterogeneity and sticky wages but flexible prices. Monopolistically competitive firms included in the model vary in productivity, as in Melitz (2003). Relatively unproductive firms exit the market due to the existence of fixed production costs. Market entry is free but associated with sunk entry costs in terms of output, leading to zero profits in the aggregate. An increasing number of firms, i.e., stronger competition (e.g., after a positive productivity shock), has two consequences. First, an individual firm must be relatively more productive to remain in the market, i.e., the cut-off productivity level a firm must reach rises. This leads to an increase in economy-wide average productivity, which can be interpreted as total factor productivity (TFP). Second, the higher cut-off productivity level makes market entry less attractive because the probability of exiting of the market increases; however, the cost of market entry also decreases due to the increase in total economy-wide average productivity.[31] Depending on which of these two effects dominate, the model results in an acceleration or deceleration effect

The model setup is used to show the quantitative relevance of the described interaction between variations in the number of firms and in TFP. Based on this

[30]Following the reasoning described in Bilbiie et al. (2007), we treat the word "firm" as a synonym for the terms "product" (or product bundle) or "producer", as this convention is customary in the related literature. The term may refer to product lines (producing a specific good or bundle) governed by independent managers and their pricing decisions within existing firms.

[31]This lower entry costs would potentially generate more entry, leading in turn again to more competition.

specification, a 1% positive technology shock leads to an approximately 1.3% increase in TFP. In comparing second moments, over 50% of the variation in the economy-wide average productivity can be explained by the propagated endogenous mechanism resulting from increasing competition.

The standard real business cycle (RBC) framework does not provide a sufficiently quantitatively important amplification mechanism and must therefore rely on highly volatile exogenous technology shocks to replicate observed aggregate economic activity volatility.[32] Our paper builds on a rapidly growing body of literature that considers firm entry and exit decisions as a potential cause of exogenous shock amplification that may help overcoming the abovementioned shortcomings of standard RBC models.[33] We contribute to this literature by describing an additional channel that is based on a principle of quantitative trade theory that firms are heterogeneous in productivity.[34] To our best knowledge, the present study provides the first attempt to incorporate this feature into the standard DSGE framework to explain potential amplification impacts of net business formation in interaction with heterogeneous productivity. Indeed, when matching key second moments of the US business cycle, our model reports values that correspond closely with data and that outperform standard RBC models as well as comparable models that include endogenous entry.

Due to the new Keynesian nature of our model, we also analyze the role of stabilizing monetary policies. Our model suggests a direct impact of monetary policy on production costs, as fixed costs must be paid in advance with money borrowed from the household sector. Thus, higher interest rates increase the cut-off productivity level that a firm must reach to produce as well as the costs of market entry, leading to less competition and fewer producing firms. In fact, these

[32]See, for example, Hall (1988), Cogley and Nason (1995), Burnside et al. (1993), and Rotemberg and Woodford (1996).

[33]See section 3.2 for a detailed discussion of the relevant literature.

[34]See, for example, Melitz (2003), Bergin and Glick (2007), Arkolakis et al. (2008), or Melitz and Ottaviano (2008). Helpman (2006) provides a general overview.

two phenomena have opposite effects on TFP, and the latter dominates according to our calibration. This transmission mechanism may also impact optimal policies pursued by a central bank.

The remainder of this chapter is organized as follows. Section 3.2 provides a short overview of the relevant literature related to our model. Section 3.3 introduces the theoretical model and describes the corresponding economic mechanisms. In section 3.4, we analyze the model dynamics and discuss the implications of TFP variation decomposition with respect to exogenous technology shocks and amplifications that are endogenously generated from the model. Furthermore, second-moment conditions are listed and compared with the data and similar models. The role of monetary policies in our framework is also discussed in section 3.5. Finally, section 3.6 provides the conclusions of this chapter.

3.2 Review of related literature

Several contributions to the existing literature propose an endogenous amplification mechanism of (technology) shocks. An important branch is related to the labor market. In such papers, the labor market is respectively characterized by frictions. For example, an early work by Howitt (1988) shows that costly labor searches can be a source of real rigidity, leading to an amplification of output shocks. Burnside et al. (1993) develop a model for labor hoarding and test it with post-war US data. The authors conclude that a significant proportion of Solow residual movement can be explained through their model.[35] Search-matching models also provide a helpful extension of the classical RBC framework, as shown by Andolfatto (1996). Den Haan et al. (2000) advance this model via endogenous job destruction.

Literature that highlights the impact of imperfect competition on business cycles is also relevant to the current study. Most of these contributions use variations

[35]See also Burnside and Eichenbaum (1996) for a general enhancement of the model.

in markup to explain business cycle patterns. However, not all papers in this stream of literature assume variations in the number of firms. Rotemberg and Woodford (1992) develop a model for oligopolistic industries, i.e., each industry in the model economy is populated by a fixed number of firms. Thus, shocks can affect implicit collusion between firms and can thus affect the markup. Galí (1994) also presents a model with a fixed number of firms in which each firm sells its product to either other firms (for capital building) or consumers. Variations in these two sources of demand can lead to variations in the markup. An alternative channel is also presented by Edmond and Veldkamp (2009). In their paper, countercyclical variations in income distribution impact markups because higher income dispersion lowers the price elasticity of demand.

However, several papers assume variations in the number of firms to reproduce variations in the markup. Cook (2001) shows that market entry after expansionary shocks creates efficiency gains in oligopolistic or monopolistic markets that act as an amplification mechanism. Devereux et al. (1996) focus on the positive effect of specialization and economies of scale on productivity after an increase in variety. Jaimovich and Floetotto (2008) present a model that not only relates demand price elasticity to the number of competitors in a monopolistic competition framework but also provides an empirical estimation regarding the impact of variation of net business formations on TFP variation.

The structural model presented here largely builds on Bilbiie et al. (2012).[36] Although this model also proposes endogenous producer entry and exit, its amplification mechanism stems from the slow response of the number of producers. This is because the only reason for a firm to leave the market is an exogenous

[36]This also implies that our work is related to the variety-based endogenous growth literature (see, e.g., Aghion and Saint-Paul (1991)), as illustrated by Bilbiie et al. (2012): "Just as the RBC model is a discrete-time, stochastic, general equilibrium version of the exogenous growth model that abstracts from growth to focus on business cycles, our model can be viewed as a discrete-time, stochastic, general equilibrium version of variety-based, endogenous growth models that abstracts from endogenous growth" (p. 308).

death shock. The authors also show that their mechanism is applicable to both constant and variable markups (modeled using either CES or translog preferences). Our work adopts the main principles of Bilbiie et al. (2012) and shares its basic conclusions, although it extends their approach by rendering firm entry and exit decisions endogenous.[37]

We also study the potential impact of monetary policy by following a monetary framework similar to that of the Bilbiie et al. (2012) model published by Bilbiie et al. (2007), although our modeling approach is different.[38] Other studies have also analyzed the relevance of monetary policy in the presence of endogenous entry. Bergin and Corsetti (2008) empirically estimate that monetary policy has a significant impact on net business formation. The authors argue that stabilizing monetary policy may cause more firms to enter as uncertainty declines. Berentsen and Waller (2009) present a model in which monetary policy can prevent the economy from excessive (due to congestion externality) entry. Bilbiie et al. (2014) argue that inflation can help stabilize markup variations. Similar reasoning is used by Lewis (2013). In her model, which incorporates sticky wages and cash-in-advance constraints, as we do, inflation can have a stabilizing effect through its impact on the real wage rate.

3.3 The model

This section provides a detailed description of the model economy and corresponding equilibrium conditions. The production component of the model can be interpreted as a dynamic enhancement of the basic Melitz (2003) model for closed economies. Producers of differentiated final goods must pay market entry and pro-

[37]Related to our approach, in the sense that firm heterogeneity and thus endogenous entry and exit are also assumed, is the paper by Campbell (1998) who applies a vintage capital model that does not include monopolistic competition.

[38]In particular, we work with sticky wages, as in Erceg et al. (2000), rather than sticky prices, and as described above, we assume heterogeneous productivity.

duction fixed costs before production can take place. To meet this requirement, firms must borrow money from households, which directly impacts monetary policies on firm production considerations. Households consume, save capital and work. However, they must also bear a sticky nominal wage rate, as shown in Erceg et al. (2000).

3.3.1 Input good production

Production involves a three-stage process. In the first stage, a perfectly competitive input good production sector combines capital and labor to produce a common input good, Γ_t, for the production of intermediate goods. Outputs supplied by this sector are[39]

$$\Gamma_{t+1} = K_t^{\alpha} L_t^{1\ \alpha}, \tag{3.1}$$

with $\alpha \in [0, 1]$. This implies that a unit of an input good produced during period t can only be used for the production of intermediate goods during the subsequent period.[40] Furthermore, labor input is given by

$$L_t = \left[\int_0^1 l_t(j)^{\rho^w} dj \right]^{\frac{1}{\rho^w}}, \tag{3.2}$$

representing total labor demand. $l_t(j)$ is the labor input during period t by workers specialized in type $j \in [0, 1]$, and $0 < \rho^w < 1$ represents the substitution parameter for labor input.[41] Firms take the nominal wage rate of each labor type, $W_t(j)$, as given. Thus, simultaneous cost minimization considerations by firms lead to the following expression for the aggregate wage rate:

$$W_t = \left[\int_0^1 W_t(j)^{\frac{\rho^w}{1\ \rho^w}} dj \right]^{\frac{1\ \rho^w}{\rho^w}}. \tag{3.3}$$

---

[39] Productivity is normalized to one, as this is strictly a scale factor.

[40] This intuitive view simply shows that an input good must be produced *before* it may be used for further processing. Similar approaches are applied by Bernanke et al. (1999) and Iacoviello (2005).

[41] See, e.g., DiCecio (2009).

Furthermore, capital must be rented during each period at a common (real) rental rate, q_t. As we assume perfect competition, the price of the input good (denoted as Υ_t) equals its total (real) marginal cost, i.e., $\Upsilon_t := \frac{q_t^{\alpha}(W_t/P_t)^{1-\alpha}}{\alpha^{\alpha}(1-\alpha)^{(1-\alpha)}}$.

3.3.2 Intermediate and final good production

The production of intermediate goods is characterized by a continuum of imperfect substitutes indexed by $\omega \in \Omega$, where Ω represents the mass of potentially available goods. Intermediate goods, $y_t(\omega)$, are combined into a final good, Y_t, as in Dixit and Stiglitz (1977), i.e.,

$$Y_t = \left[\int_{\omega_t \in \Omega} y_t(\omega)^{\rho} d\omega\right]^{\frac{1}{\rho}}, \tag{3.4}$$

where $0 < \rho < 1$ is the time-invariant constant substitution parameter. Producers of final goods behave competitively. Denoting $p_t(\omega)$ as the price of a single intermediate good, the price of the final good is given by

$$P_t = \left[\int_{\omega_t \in \Omega} p_t(\omega)^{\frac{\rho}{1-\rho}} d\omega\right]^{\frac{1-\rho}{\rho}}. \tag{3.5}$$

Optimization considerations of the final good producers result in the typical conditional demand for each intermediate good,

$$y_t(\omega) = \left(\frac{P_t}{p_t(\omega)}\right)^{\frac{1}{1-\rho}} Y_t. \tag{3.6}$$

Each intermediate good producer selects a different variety, ω. Input good, Γ_t, is the only necessary production factor in a constant-return-to-scale production function. All firms face the same time-invariant fixed cost, $f > 0$, in terms of input good, Γ_t, but under different marginal costs (for a symmetric variety), which is modeled by different factor productivity, denoted as $\varphi > 0$. Firms draw their initial productivity, φ, from a common distribution, $g_t(\varphi)$, which is defined over interval

$[\varphi_t^{min}, \infty)$.[42] The respective continuous cumulative distribution is $G_t(\varphi)$. The minimum productivity level, φ_t^{min}, can be interpreted as the general technology level within the economy that is subject to innovation and upon which every entering firm can build. Thus, it is assumed that

$$\varphi_t^{min} = \left(\varphi_{t\ 1}^{min}\right)^{\zeta} \left(\overline{\varphi}^{min}\right)^{1\ \ \zeta} \varepsilon_t, \tag{3.7}$$

i.e., φ_t^{min} follows a first-order auto-regressive process with a persistence parameter, $\zeta \in [0, 1]$, and a lognormal distributed innovation, ε, with mean one and standard deviation σ_ε. $\overline{\varphi}^{min}$ represents the steady state value of the minimum productivity level.

The total output per intermediate good producer is given by $y_t(\varphi) = \varphi(\Gamma_t(\varphi) - f)$, where $\Gamma_t(\varphi)$ is the mass of input good demanded by a firm with productivity φ. Fixed costs, f, are subject to a cash-in-advance (CIA) constraint. One may consider this as a basic investment in each period that must be paid before production takes place. Firms must borrow the necessary money from the households at a common interest rate, i_t.[43]

These conditions produce the following profit maximizing function for an individual firm (whose profit in period t is denoted as $\phi_t(\varphi)$) during a given period:

$$\max_{p_t(\varphi)} \phi_t(\varphi) = p_t(\varphi) y_t(\varphi) - \frac{\Upsilon_t}{\varphi} y_t(\varphi) - (1 + i_t)\Upsilon_t f. \tag{3.8}$$

Using the demand function (3.6), this yields the following pricing rule:

$$p_t(\varphi) = \frac{\Upsilon_t}{\varphi \rho}, \tag{3.9}$$

---

[42] Because the lower boundary of the restricted domain is time dependent, the distribution as a whole becomes time dependent as well. However, we assume that central moments of the basic distribution remain constant, i.e., the actual distribution is conditional.

[43] This approach to CIA modeling follows Chu and Cozzi (2014). However, in their paper, the CIA applies to a R&D sector only.

where $1/\rho$ is the profit-maximizing markup chosen by each firm. Thus, the total profits for a single producer of intermediate goods, denoted as $\phi_t(\varphi)$, facing a certain productivity level, φ, during period t are given by

$$\phi_t(\varphi) = P_t^{\frac{1}{1-\rho}} C_t(1-\rho)\left(\frac{\varphi\rho}{\Upsilon_t}\right)^{\frac{\rho}{1-\rho}} - (1+i_t)\Upsilon_t f. \tag{3.10}$$

3.3.3 Aggregation

During each period, t, an equilibrium characterized by a mass, M_t, of intermediate good producers is present. Given this firm mass, M_t, and distribution $g_t(\varphi)$, the price and output of the final good are given by

$$P_t = \left[\int_{\varphi_t^{min}}^{\infty} p_t(\varphi)^{\frac{\rho}{1-\rho}} M_t g_t(\varphi) d\varphi\right]^{\frac{1-\rho}{\rho}}, \tag{3.11}$$

$$Y_t = \left[\int_{\varphi_t^{min}}^{\infty} y_t(\varphi)^{\rho} M_t g_t(\varphi) d\varphi\right]^{\frac{1}{\rho}}. \tag{3.12}$$

After including the pricing rule (3.9), this can be written as

$$P_t = M_t^{\frac{\rho-1}{\rho}} p_t(\tilde{\varphi}_t) = \frac{\Upsilon_t}{M_t^{\frac{1-\rho}{\rho}} \rho\tilde{\varphi}_t}, \tag{3.13}$$

$$Y_t = M_t^{1/\rho} y_t(\tilde{\varphi}_t), \tag{3.14}$$

where

$$\tilde{\varphi}_t := \left[\int_{\varphi_t^{min}}^{\infty} \varphi^{\frac{\rho}{1-\rho}} g_t(\varphi) d\varphi\right]^{\frac{1-\rho}{\rho}}, \tag{3.15}$$

denotes the weighted average productivity level of producing firms. As shown by Melitz (2003), $\tilde{\varphi}_t$ comprises all relevant information on the distribution of productivity and can be treated as a weighted average productivity that implies the same aggregate outcome as an economy with the same number of firms that share, in contrast to the model at hand, the same productivity level $\tilde{\varphi}_t$. This condition allows us to treat $\tilde{\varphi}_t$ as measure of TFP.[44]

[44]In what follows, we therefore use the terms "TFP" and "weighted average productivity" interchangeably.

3.3.4 Free entry and zero cut-off productivity condition

In each period, there is an unbounded pool of prospective entrants into the market of intermediate goods. To produce, firms must pay in each period an initial (and subsequently sunk) investment, $f_e > 0$, in terms of the final good, Y_t, which must also be paid in advance using cash borrowed from households at the common interest rate, i_t. After paying the initial investment, firms draw their productivity level, φ. If this level is sufficiently low that prospective profit is negative, a firm immediately exits without producing. Following the reasoning presented by Bernanke et al. (1999), this procedure is repeated during each period, i.e., even a firm that produced during period t must repay the initial investment cost, f_e, and draw a new productivity level, φ, in period $t+1$, independent of its previous productivity level.[45] Thus, as in Bernanke et al. (1999), one may interpret φ as a form of idiosyncratic individual productivity *shock* that affects firms during each period.[46] Furthermore, sunk entry costs, f_e, may be considered as general costs of regulation or the like in this context. The basic insight of the model would also hold when assuming that firms may maintain productivity status after entering and before exiting the market again.[47] However, such an approach would only result in a stronger persistence of the weighted average productivity parameter, $\tilde{\varphi}_t$ (as the shape of the incumbent firm productivity distribution would become time-dependent).

Due to the existence of fixed costs, f, there must exist a minimal level of productivity, denoted as φ_t^*, that a firm must draw to make positive profits. We assume that $\varphi_t^* \geqslant \varphi_t^{min}$ $\forall$ t is always true. Any entering firm that draws a productivity level of $\varphi < \varphi_t^*$ would never produce and then immediately exit the market. Using the individual firm profit function (3.10), we obtain the following relation for this

[45] Thus, random variable φ is i.i.d. across time and firms.

[46] There may also be an aggregate common productivity level that we may disregard without loss of generality.

[47] This may occur when firms are hit by dead shocks, as described in Melitz (2003), or when firms are no longer profitable.

cut-off productivity level:

$$\varphi_t^* = \left(\frac{\rho}{1-\rho} \frac{(1+i_t) f M_t^{1/\rho} \tilde{\varphi}_t^{\frac{1}{1-\rho}}}{Y_t} \right)^{\frac{1-\rho}{\rho}}. \tag{3.16}$$

The cut-off productivity level, φ_t^*, increases with not only the (gross) fixed cost level, but also the number of firms, M_t, and weighted average productivity level, $\tilde{\varphi}_t$. The impact of the latter two variables can be understood as a consequence of stronger competition within the economy. In contrast, higher output of the final good, Y_t, which can be understood as a higher level of demand, lowers the productivity level that a firm must achieve. Note that φ_t^* is independent of the input good price, Υ_t (which represents the marginal costs of intermediate good producers). This is a direct consequence of the CES specification for the demand for intermediate goods, which implies that an increase in marginal costs is mirrored by the price level on a one-to-one basis.[48]

Because firms with productivity levels below φ_t^* do not produce, the distribution of productivity within the economy becomes conditional. Thus, the weighted average productivity, $\tilde{\varphi}_t$, depends on the cut-off productivity level as follows:

$$\tilde{\varphi}_t = \left[\int_{\varphi_t^*}^{\infty} \varphi^{\frac{\rho}{1-\rho}} \frac{g_t(\varphi)}{1 - G_t(\varphi_t^*)} d\varphi \right]^{\frac{1-\rho}{\rho}}. \tag{3.17}$$

We generally assume that the distribution $g_t(\varphi)$ ensures that $\tilde{\varphi}_t$ is finite during each period, t.[49]

Each incumbent intermediate good producer that draws a productivity level, φ, above the cut-off productivity level, φ_t^*, makes positive profit. Assuming that a firm produces after having paid entry investment fixed costs, f_e, the expected profit, denoted as $\overline{\phi}_t$, is given by

[48] See, e.g., Bilbiie et al. (2012).

[49] Thus, according to Melitz (2003), the $\frac{\rho}{1-\rho}$th moment of $g_t(\varphi)$ cannot be infinite.

$$
\begin{aligned}
\overline{\phi}_t &\equiv E[\phi_t(\varphi) \mid \varphi > \varphi_t^*] \\
&= \int_{\varphi_t^*}^{\infty} \left[P_t^{\frac{1}{1-\rho}} Y_t(1-\rho) \left(\frac{\varphi \rho}{\Upsilon_t} \right)^{\frac{\rho}{1-\rho}} - (1+i_t)\,\Upsilon_t f \right] \frac{g_t(\varphi)}{1-G_t(\varphi_t^*)} d\varphi \\
&= \frac{1-\rho}{\rho} \frac{\Upsilon_t Y_t}{M_t^{1/\rho} \tilde{\varphi}_t} - (1+i_t)\Upsilon_t f.
\end{aligned}
\tag{3.18}
$$

As the number of prospective entrants is unbounded, firms enter until the expected profit, $\overline{\phi}_t$, equals the cost of market entry. These costs are given by $\frac{(1+i_t)P_t f_e}{1-G_t(\varphi_t^*)}$. The adjustment factor $1/(1-G_t(\varphi_t^*))$ represents the risk premium as firms drawing a productivity level below φ_t^* would not produce. After rearranging the resulting free-entry condition, $\overline{\phi}_t = \frac{(1+i_t)P_t f_e}{1-G_t(\varphi_t^*)}$, and using the price level definition (3.14), we receive the total number of firms during period t given by the following relation:

$$
\frac{f_e M_t}{1-G_t(\varphi_t^*)} + f M_t^{1/\rho} \tilde{\varphi}_t \rho = \frac{(1-\rho)Y_t}{1+i_t}. \tag{3.19}
$$

For each period's equilibrium component, aggregate profit must be equal to the aggregated fixed entry cost. This requirement is an immediate consequence from equation (3.19) as $M_t \overline{\phi}_t = M_t \frac{(1+i_t)P_t f_e}{1-G_t(\varphi_t^*)}$. One may assume that a fund, in which all firms are pooled (including firms that never produce due to exceedingly low productivity levels) and to which all profits thus flow, is responsible for the payment of fixed entry costs.

Equations (3.16)-(3.19) disclose the endogenous impact that competition can have on economy-wide productivity. A larger number of firms, M_t, leads to an increase in cut-off productivity, φ_t^*, because a firm must be relatively more productive to make positive profits. Thus, the weighted average productivity, $\tilde{\varphi}_t$, i.e., the overall productivity of the economy also increases. This trend has two effects. A more productive economy rises income and demand levels (i.e., the potential profit possibilities of entering) but also lowers the general price level and thus the costs of market entry. Hence, both channels create an incentive for even more firms to enter. However, higher cut-off productivity decreases the likelihood of producing at all after individual productivity levels are drawn, preventing firms from entering. Given that the first effects have a greater impact, e.g., effects following a productivity shock, an amplification mechanism of competition for weighted average productivity, which can be regarded as TFP in our model, is established.

3.3.5 Total output

From equation (3.14), we know that the total output of the final good is given by $Y_t = M_t^{1/\rho} y_t(\tilde{\varphi}_t)$. Furthermore, we can conclude that $\frac{\Gamma_t}{M_t} = \Gamma_t(\tilde{\varphi}_t)$, i.e., that a firm drawing during a given period, t, a productivity level $\varphi = \tilde{\varphi}_t$ demands a precisely average share of the input goods available.[50] Thus, the total output of the final good is given by

$$Y_t = M_t^{\frac{1\ \rho}{\rho}} \tilde{\varphi}_t \Gamma_t - M_t^{1/\rho} \tilde{\varphi}_t f - \frac{M_t f_e}{1 - G_t(\varphi_t^*)}. \tag{3.20}$$

This concludes the description of the production sector. We generally assume that macroeconomic shocks and fixed costs are sufficiently minor to ensure positive outputs in each period, t.

3.3.6 Households and preferences

The economy is populated by a mass of infinitely living households that are normalized to one. Each household consists of a continuum of members that are each specialized in a specific labor type, j. Individual utility is assumed to be given by

$$U(C_t(j), L_t(j)) = E_0 \sum_{t=0}^{\infty} \beta^t \left[ln \left(C_t(j) - h\overline{C}_{t\ 1} \right) - \chi \frac{L_t(j)^{1+\eta}}{1+\eta} \right], \tag{3.21}$$

where $C_t(j)$ is the consumption of the final good during period t, $\overline{C}_{t\ 1}$ is the lagged aggregate consumption by the household (taken as given by each household member), and $h \in [0,1]$ is the habit weight. $\beta \in [0,1]$ is the discount factor, $\chi > 0$

[50]This is because M_t symmetric firms sharing the same productivity level $\tilde{\varphi}_t$ would generate the same aggregated outcome for a given period, t. See Melitz (2003) for a discussion.

is the preference shifter, and $\eta \geqslant 0$ governs the Frisch labor supply elasticity. We allow for (external) habit formation, as in Galí et al. (2012). This is generally the case for related dynamic stochastic general equilibrium models involving money, e.g., in Bouakez et al. (2005), Smets and Wouters (2007) and DiCecio (2009). Following Ngo (2014), the aim of habit formation is to generate a higher attentiveness of households for consumption smoothing as the Euler equation becomes also backward looking.[51] Thus, consumption becomes also a state variable, producing a hump-shaped pattern in the impulse response function of consumption and other related variables, which is more in line with empirical findings.

Following Merz (1995), we assume full risk sharing across household members, i.e., household period utility is the relevant decision object and corresponds to the member utility integral. Thus, the representative household seeks to maximize

$$U(C_t, L_t(j)) = E_0 \sum_{t=0}^{\infty} \beta^t \left[\log\left(C_t - h\overline{C}_{t\ 1}\right) - \chi \int_0^1 \frac{L_t(j)^{1+\eta}}{1+\eta} dj \right], \tag{3.22}$$

subject to a sequence of budget constraints,

$$\begin{aligned} C_t + K_{t+1} + \mu_t + b_t \leqslant & \int_0^1 \frac{W_t(j)}{P_t} L_t(j) dj \\ & + ((1-\delta) + q_t)K_t + (\mu_{t\ 1} + (1+i_{t\ 1})b_{t\ 1})\frac{P_{t\ 1}}{P_t} + \Pi_t + \tau_t, \end{aligned} \tag{3.23}$$

where K_t denotes the value of capital stock[52], δ is the depreciation rate for capital, μ_t is real money holding, Π_t is the real profit of the corporate sector remitted to households, and τ_t is a lump-sum transfer from the central bank (which may be positive or negative). b_t is the real amount of money borrowed by firms to finance fixed production and entry costs (from the household perspective, these may be interpreted as bonds), and i_t is the known nominal net interest rate paid for this lending (which is yielded from time t to $t+1$). The initial capital stock is

[51] cp. equation (3.25) below. See Dotsey et al. (1999) for a detailed motivation of habit formation.
[52] It is implied that the capital stock must be built up from the final good.

given and equals $K_0 > 0$. Furthermore, households face a CIA constraint, which is given by[53]

$$C_t + b_t \leqslant (\mu_{t\ 1} + (1 + i_{t\ 1})b_{t\ 1})\frac{P_{t\ 1}}{P_t} + \tau_t. \tag{3.24}$$

The CIA constraint implies that households must decide during each period whether to spend money for consumption or lend money to the (intermediate good) production sector. Finally, all relevant transversality conditions are assumed to apply. Thus, the respective Euler equation for optimal intertemporal consumption is

$$\frac{1}{C_t - h\overline{C}_{t\ 1}} = \beta E_t \left[\frac{1 + i_t}{\pi_{t+1}\left(C_{t+1} - h\overline{C}_t\right)} \right], \tag{3.25}$$

where $\pi_{t+1} \equiv \frac{P_{t+1}}{P_t}$. Optimal capital accumulation can be interpreted as an arbitrage condition that implies that the real gross interest rate must equal the capital gross rental rate. Thus, we end up with the following simple Fisher equation:

$$E_t \left[\frac{1 + i_{t+1}}{\pi_{t+1}} \right] = (1 - \delta) + E_t \left[q_{t+1} \right]. \tag{3.26}$$

As the production sector for input goods is perfectly competitive, the capital rental rate must equal its marginal productivity value, i.e.,

$$q_t = \alpha \left(\frac{L_t}{K_t} \right)^{1\ \alpha} = \alpha \frac{\Gamma_{t+1}}{K_t}. \tag{3.27}$$

The final good, Y_t, can only be used for capital accumulation and consumption, i.e., it must hold that

$$Y_t = C_t - K_{t+1} + (1 - \delta)K_t, \tag{3.28}$$

which may also simply be described as the market-clearing condition.

[53]As mentioned, the approach follows Chu and Cozzi (2014), in which money must be lent to the R&D sector only.

3.3.7 Wage setting and labor supply

Nominal wages are subject to inertia, as in Erceg et al. (2000). This may be attributable to that fact that we employ long-term wage contracts, e.g., due to union power. Each type of labor can adjust wages in each period based on constant, time-independent probability $1-\gamma$, i.e., wage setting follows the formalism provided by Calvo (1983). Thus, a fraction γ of workers work under unchanging wages during a given period. Hence, the aggregate wage index expression is given by

$$W_t = W_{t-1}^{\gamma} W_t^{*(1-\gamma)}, \tag{3.29}$$

where W_t^* is the wage rate chosen by a labor type that can adjust its wage rate (all labor types that can re-optimize during a given period choose the same wage rate). As described by Galí (2011), this approach is practiced to maximize household (rather than individual) utility subject to a sequence of isoelastic demand schedules for a specific labor type. The respective first-order condition from this optimization is given by[54]

$$\sum_{k=0}^{\infty}(\beta\gamma)^k E_t\left[\frac{L_{t+k|t}}{C_{t+k}}\left(\frac{W_t^*}{P_{t+k}} - \frac{1}{\rho^w} MRS_{t+k|t}\right)\right] = 0, \tag{3.30}$$

where $MRS_{t+k|t} \equiv \chi L_{t+k|t}^{\eta}\left(C_{t+k} - hC_{t+k-1}\right)(1+i_{t+k})$ is the marginal rate of substitution between consumption and labor and $1/\rho^w$ is the desired markup in case of a flexible wage setting, i.e., also in the steady state. Log-linearizing the above relation yields the approximate wage setting rule[55],

$$w_t^* = \varrho^w + (1-\beta\gamma)\sum_{k=0}^{\infty}(\beta\gamma)^k E_t\left[mrs_{t+k|t} + p_{t+k}\right], \tag{3.31}$$

where $\varrho^w \equiv \log(1/\rho^w)$. Combining this with the (log-linearized) equation (3.29) yields the Philips-curve equation for the wage rate,

$$\pi_t^w = \beta E_t\left[\pi_{t+1}^w\right] - \lambda^w\left(w_t - p_t - mrs_t - \varrho^w\right), \tag{3.32}$$

[54]For details on the derivation, see Erceg et al. (2000).

[55]Logarithmic values are hereafter denoted in small letters.

where $mrs_t \equiv \chi + \eta l_t + \log(c_t - hc_{t-1}) + \log(1 + i_t)$, $\pi^w \equiv w_t - w_{t-1}$ denotes wage rate inflation, and

$$\lambda^w \equiv \frac{(1-\gamma)(1-\beta\gamma)}{\gamma(1+\eta\frac{\rho^w}{1-\rho^w})}. \tag{3.33}$$

As it would follow a standard new Keynesian Philips-curve, the current wage inflation rate depends positively on the expected single period ahead wage inflation value and negatively on the average current wage deviation (markup) from its desired level. The model considers sticky wages rather than sticky prices, although this would be the standard approach used in the new Keynesian literature.[56] The sticky wage approach is used because prices, in contrast to wages, are not equal across firms. However, as Huang and Liu (2002) notes, the two approaches to monetary policy persistence effect calculation provide similar outcomes. Furthermore, the sticky wage approach is considered to produce more realistic patterns.

3.3.8 The central bank

The last component of the model economy describes the behavior of the central bank, which follows a simple interest rate rule,[57]

$$i_t = i^{1-\xi} i_{t-1}^{\xi} \left[\left(\frac{Y_t}{Y}\right)^{\theta_y} \left(\frac{\pi_t}{\pi}\right)^{\theta_\pi} \right]^{1-\xi}, \tag{3.34}$$

where variables without time subscripts denote steady state values, $\xi \in [0,1]$ is the interest rate inertia parameter, $\theta_y > 0$ is the weighting parameter on the output gap, and $\theta_\pi > 0$ is the parameter representing the desire for price stability. The central bank strictly follows this rule. Note that the interest rate rule can be expressed equivalently in dependence of the net or the gross interest rate.

The Taylor rule concludes the model description.

56 Following the work of Erceg et al. (2000), a substantial component of the literature also applies models that contain both sticky prices and wages.

57 The central bank can enforce every aspired interest rate via monetary transfer, τ_t.

3.3.9 Parametrization of the technology distribution

The described model can be applied to any productivity draw distribution, $G_t(\varphi)$, that fulfills the described requirements regarding moments. However, to make the model solvable, we apply a specific parametrization scheme for the distribution. Following Melitz and Ottaviano (2008), Arkolakis et al. (2008) and Atkeson and Burstein (2010), among others, we assume that productivity is Pareto-distributed, i.e., $G_t(\varphi) = 1 - \left(\frac{\varphi_t^{min}}{\varphi}\right)^{\kappa}$, where κ is a shape parameter. To guarantee finite moments, we assume that $\kappa > \frac{\rho}{1-\rho} \wedge \kappa > 1$. Thus, the weighted average productivity, $\tilde{\varphi}_t$, becomes explicitly defined,[58]

$$\tilde{\varphi}_t = \left(1 - \frac{\rho}{(1-\rho)\kappa}\right)^{\frac{\rho-1}{\rho}} \varphi_t^*. \tag{3.35}$$

This implies that the relation between the cut-off productivity level, φ_t^*, and weighted average productivity, $\tilde{\varphi}_t$, is linear. This result allows us to treat the minimum productivity level, φ_t^{min}, as the general technology level without restrictions because the transmission of shocks would be, ceteris paribus, linear as well (i.e., the distribution induces no endogenous reaction).

3.3.10 Equilibrium and model dynamics

Absent shocks, the model exhibits a unique stable equilibrium given that fixed production costs, f, fixed entry costs, f_e, and productivity distribution, $g_t(\varphi)$, ensure a positive output level. The equilibrium is an allocation $\{K_t, L_t, \Gamma_t, Y_t, C_t, b_t\}_{t=0}^{\infty}$ together with a sequence of values $\{W_t, W_t^*, q_t, P_t, \varphi_t^*, \tilde{\varphi}_t, \Upsilon_t\}_{t=0}^{\infty}$, satisfying equations (3.1) to (3.34) and the sequence of technology shocks, $\{\varepsilon_t\}$, together with the relevant transversality conditions. In a perfect foresight, zero-inflation steady state, it holds that $1+i = 1/\beta$, $\varphi^{min} = \overline{\varphi}^{min}$, $q = \frac{1}{\beta} - (1-\delta)$, and $\frac{W}{P} = \frac{W^*}{P} = \frac{\chi L^{\eta} C(1+i)}{\rho^{w}}$, whereas all other relations are the same as in the dynamic case.[59]

[58]cp. equation (3.17).

[59]Time subscripts are omitted to denote steady state variables.

Due to fundamental non-linearity, the model is not directly solvable and is thus linearized around its steady state. The complete linearized system can be found in appendix 3.A. This system is then numerically solved using the Dynare-toolkit.[60]

3.4 Model estimations

In this section, we investigate the properties of our model via numerical examples. In particular, we compute impulse response functions to a productivity shock. Furthermore, we compare the second moments generated by our model with those generated through standard RBC models and the model developed by Bilbiie et al. (2007) as well as the moments generated through US data.

3.4.1 Calibration of parameters

When calibrating the model parameters, we generally choose values that are propagated throughout the standard monetary/real business cycle and quantitative trade literature. The latter is used because it represents the basis of the heterogeneous productivity model. We calibrate the model to the US economy. The aspired time unit is one quarter. We generally distinguish between the household sector, production sector, and Taylor rule parameters.

As in most studies that follow the standard RBC framework proposed by King and Rebelo (1999), we set the time discount factor, β, to 0.99, implying an average yearly nominal interest rate of approximately 4%, as this value corresponds to pre-crisis US data. The capital depreciation rate, δ, is set to 0.025, implying a yearly exogenous capital destruction rate of 10%. These values are also used in all other sources on which we rely in our calibration. For the habit coefficient, h, we choose a value of 0.6 in accordance with Ngo (2014). According to this author, this value implies a rather moderate habit formation compared to values used in

[60] See www.dynare.org or Adjemian et al. (2011).

earlier theoretical works that apply this preference setting. However, the value corresponds well with recent empirical findings.

Regarding labor supply elasticity, η, a broader range of values has been used in the literature. However, Huang and Liu (2002) clearly state that most empirical studies set η to a value of 2. We follow this proposition, as major findings are not particularly sensitive to the calibration of this parameter. The quarterly probability of wage adjustment is taken from DiCecio (2009) and is assumed to be 27% (i.e., γ is set to 0.73). This value is approximately equal to the mean of estimations used in Galí (2011). It also implies that, on average, wages are adjusted approximately once a year, which is in line with most wage contracts.

The χ parameter is not freely calibrated but instead determined under the steady state such that the value of L equals the average US labor force during the 2003-2013 period.[61] This procedure is proposed by Melitz and Redding (2014). This measure also allows for the normalization of fixed production and entry costs (f and f_e, respectively) to one, as these variables would only act as scaling factors.

Regarding the production sector, we assume a typical (also empirically supported) capital share of one third, i.e., α is set to 0.33, as in King and Rebelo (1999) and virtually all relevant literature. The elasticity of substitution between intermediate goods, ρ, is set to 0.75, as in Bilbiie et al. (2012), implying a markup of approximately one third above marginal costs, which is somewhat higher than that applied in the older literature. However, this reported calibration is based on empirical findings by Bernard et al. (2003).[62] For substitution elasticity between labor types, we rely on Galí et al. (2012), who report (in accordance with similar work by these authors) a value of 0.8 for ρ^w.

Parameters related to the productivity distribution are taken from Melitz and Redding (2014), which is understood as the current standard source for models

[61] Corresponding employment data are provided by the US Bureau of Labor Statistics.

[62] A similar value is used by Lewis (2009) and Melitz and Redding (2014) in a model with endogenous firm entry.

that use this feature. According to this study, empirical insights denote a shape parameter, κ, equal to 4.25. Thus, we adopt this value for our model. Regarding the persistence parameter, we follow Schmitt-Grohé and Uribe (2007), which is referenced by other papers related to the present study, e.g., Bilbiie et al. (2014). Thus, for our basic calibration, we set ζ to 0.856. Nevertheless, we rely on values used by King and Rebelo (1999) in the respective section to render the analysis of second moments comparable with other models.[63]

The final group of parameters, which are concerned with monetary policy, are based on our own estimation of the Taylor rule. This approach is commonly used throughout the new Keynesian literature. The methodological procedure follows Iacoviello (2005) with some modifications. In particular, we first calculate the relative deviation of real GDP growth, the federal fund rate and inflation from its mean for each quarter.[64] The second stage involves running a simple OLS-regression of the interest rate deviation on its own lag, real GDP deviation and inflation rate deviation for the 1984Q1-2013Q3 period.[65] Detailed results of the estimation are reported in appendix 3.B. In accordance with these results, we set ξ to 0.859, θ_y to 0.342, and θ_π to 0.406.[66]

Table 3.1 summarizes the model calibration and reports the main source of the values chosen. Model dynamics are not generally sensitive to (minor) changes in calibrated values. Based on this calibration, the steady state values of the respective variables are calculated as they appear in the linearized model using a simple numerical approximation algorithm.[67]

---

[63] cp. section 3.4.3.

[64] Using the deviation from the mean rather than the deviation from a trend complements the work of Smets and Wouters (2007).

[65] To avoid disturbances from great disinflation, we restrict the estimation to the post-1984 period.

[66] The calibrated parameters for θ_y and θ_π differ from the coefficients reported in appendix 3.B, as coefficients from the OLS-regression must be divided by $1 - \xi$ (cp. equation (3.34)).

[67] The respective code is written in MatLab® and is available upon request. Note that the nominal wage rate is assumed to be the numéraire for the steady state.

Table 3.1: Calibrated parameters for the baseline model and source.

Parameter	Description	Value	Source of calibration
Household sector			
β	Time discount factors	0.99	King and Rebelo (1999)
δ	Depreciation rate	0.025	King and Rebelo (1999)
h	Habit coefficient	0.6	Ngo (2014)
η	Labor supply elasticity	2	Huang and Liu (2002)
γ	Probability of wage persistence	0.73	DiCecio (2009)
χ	Preference shifter	0.4572	Melitz and Redding (2014)
	(s.t. L equals US labor force)		
Production sector			
α	Capital share	0.33	King and Rebelo (1999)
ρ	Elast. of subst. between products	0.75	Bilbiie et al. (2012)
ρ^w	Elast. of subst. between labor types	0.8	Galí et al. (2012)
f_e, f	Fixed costs	1	Melitz and Redding (2014)
κ	Shape parameter of the Pareto distr.	4.25	Melitz and Redding (2014)
$\overline{\varphi}^{min}$	Minimum productivity level in SS	1	Melitz and Redding (2014)
ζ	AR(1)-coefficient	0.856	Schmitt-Grohé and Uribe (2007)
Monetary Policy			
ξ	Persistence parameter of monetary policy	0.859	*Own estimations.*
θ_y	Monetary policy weight on output gap	0.342	*Own estimations.*
θ_π	Monetary policy weight on inflation	0.406	*Own estimations.*

3.4.2 Impulse responses

Standard RBC models cannot generate a sufficiently quantitatively important amplification mechanism. Thus, as shown by Jaimovich and Floetotto (2008), these models must rely on highly volatile exogenous technology shocks to account for observed fluctuations in output and other aggregated economic measures. Our model proposes a mechanism in which additional entry due to positive technology shocks leads to stronger competition. This in turn forces relatively unproductive firms to leave the market, leading to an even stronger increase in average productivity within the economy. However, can this mechanism generate a sufficient amount of additional variation to overcome the shortcomings of the standard RBC framework? The following simulation provides insights on quantitative relevance.

The presented impulse response functions (IRFs), shown in figure 3.2, illustrate the reaction of key endogenous variables to a 1% innovation to φ_t^{min}, i.e., to the minimum productivity level, as a percentage deviation from the steady state. Numbers on the horizontal axis in each panel of the figure refer to quarters after the shock. The panel on the evolution of weighted average productivity, $\tilde{\varphi}_t$, in the lower-right corner depicts the dynamic TFP response within the economy. The amplification effect becomes evident when one compares the IRF to the minimum productivity level, φ_t^{min}, in the same panel. Deviation of TFP from steady state is 31% higher than the technology shock would induce during the impact period. Due to the hump-shaped pattern of related key variables, this is somewhat weaker than the immediate impact reported by Jaimovich and Floetotto (2008) who use a RBC model with firm entry and markup variations. However, this characteristic renders the mechanism more persistent. A comparison between the mentioned IRFs (for φ_t^{min} and $\tilde{\varphi}_t$) and the IRF for the number of firms, M_t (in the lower-left panel), further reveals the relationship between the number of firms and productivity. Deviation from the steady state of weighted average productivity will be higher or lower than the deviation of the minimum productivity level depending on whether deviation of the number of firms from the steady state is negative or positive, respectively.

Based on the estimation for model dynamics following a technology shock, we can further examine variations in weighted average productivity (which we consider as TFP). We find that $var(\varphi_t^{min})/var(\tilde{\varphi}_t) = 0.44$. This result is somewhat higher than the number that is reported by Jaimovich and Floetotto (2008) for empirical analysis and implies that 56% of the variation in $\tilde{\varphi}_t$ stems from the propagated endogenous mechanism. This result implies that the impact of higher competition on the cut-off productivity level and therefore on average productivity can account for a significant share of measured (weighted) average productivity variation.

Note that the IRFs for weighted average and cut-off productivity are identical. This finding results from the linear relationship created through the Pareto distribution.

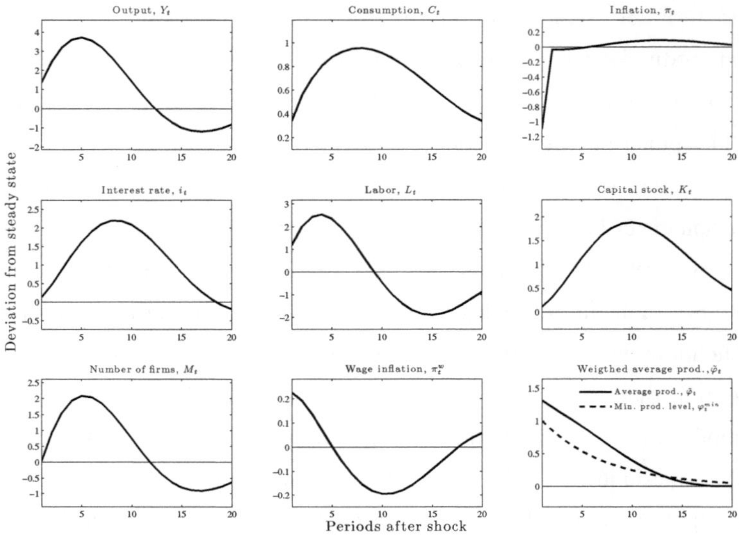

Figure 3.2: Impulse response functions I.
Percentage deviation from the steady state for key variables following a positive 1% shock to the minimum technology level. Periods refer to quarters.

The remaining IRF values shown in figure 3.2 are standard for monetary models that include habit formation and sticky wages. Consumption, C_t, reaches a maximum level after seven periods, and labor supply, L_t, reaches its maximum value after three periods. Together with capital accumulation, this explains the hump-shaped trend for the number of firms. Output, Y_t, reverts to the steady state more rapidly, whereas the persistence level is relatively strong during the first few periods due to the accumulation of capital together with a higher labor supply and the presence of more producing firms. With the exception of consumption, all economic aggregates return to the steady state in an oscillating manner.

Inflation, π_t, is strongly negative in the first period (due to supply-side shock) and remains at approximately zero thereafter. This is a typical pattern in models that include sticky wages but flexible prices. This pattern also accounts for the reaction of the interest rate, i_t, which, despite the positive shock, remains close to the steady state level during the first period and is then dominated by the reaction to output deviation. Wage inflation, π_t^w, develops in relation to output, i.e., it is positive after the initial shock and remains positive as long as the output gap increases but then becomes negative.

3.4.3 Second moments

To further evaluate properties of our model, we compute unconditional second moments for a number of central variables that our model economy generates. These moments are then compared to US data and results reported by Bilbiie et al. (2007)[68], and by King and Rebelo (1999) for the benchmark RBC model, respectively. To ensure comparability, we model persistence and productivity shock as in King and Rebelo (1999) (and also in Bilbiie et al. (2007)), i.e., we set $\zeta = 0.979$ and $\sigma_\varepsilon = 0.0072$. Following the conventions of the RBC literature and maintaining consistency with data, we compute model-implied second moments for HP-filtered variables using a smoothing parameter of 1,600.

Table 3.2 presents the results. For each variable, the first number denotes the empirical moment for US data reported by King and Rebelo (1999), and the second refers to results generated by our model. The third and fourth numbers present the results of the RBC benchmark model and Bilbiie et al. (2007) model (hereafter denoted as the BGM model), respectively.

[68]This is a version of the Bilbiie et al. (2012) model featuring sticky prices and active monetary policy. Thus, it is rather directly comparable with our framework.

Table 3.2: Comparison of second moments.

	σ_X				$corr(X_t, X_{t\ 1})$				$corr(X_t, Y_t)$			
Var. X	Data	Model	RBC	BGM	Data	Model	RBC	BGM	Data	Model	RBC	BGM
Y_t	1.81	1.81	1.39	1.36	0.84	0.80	0.72	0.70				
C_t	1.35	1.03	0.61	0.66	0.80	0.91	0.79	0.74	0.88	0.81	0.94	0.98
Invest.	5.30	5.13	4.09	5.20	0.87	0.75	0.71	0.69	0.80	0.94	0.99	0.99
L_t	1.79	0.65	0.67	0.63	0.88	0.95	0.71	0.69	0.88	0.40	0.97	0.98

Source: King and Rebelo (1999) for data and the RBC model. BGM refers to moments reported by Bilbiie et al. (2007).

Our model outperforms the standard RBC and BGM models in reproducing key moments of the US business cycle with respect to output and consumption. Output variance notably mimics patterns in the data which is a direct consequence of the amplification mechanism through TFP; the standard deviation of capital investment differs only slightly, whereas the RBC model underestimates this number and the BGM model reports a number similar to ours. Consumption variation is still somewhat underestimated, as in most business cycle models, but follows data trends more closely than the benchmark models, e.g., approximately 50% higher than the BGM model, which is a remarkable improvement. This result is primary a direct effect of the higher volatility in output but also a consequence of the model setting with sticky wages. However, with respect to autocorrelation, the model suggests, with a coefficient of 0.91, excessive persistence in consumption - a potential consequence of the sticky wage and habit formation approach applied in our model.

Unfortunately, the model does not fully reproduce labor supply properties. In particular, labor supply is exceedingly smooth relative to the data and is also much less correlated with output. This discrepancy may be attributed to the new Keynesian nature of our framework, whereas especially the fact that we rely exclusively on sticky wages (i.e., wages are relatively less volatile) reinforces this effect.

Overall, the performance of our model, given the proposed calibration that includes the estimated Taylor rule, can be viewed as a relative success. Due to the amplification mechanism, the model possesses second-moment properties that are remarkably close to the data in many respects. Thus, variation in the number of firms results in not only higher (and therefore more realistic) output variance but also higher consumption variance compared to standard RBC models. Finally, and partially due to our approach that includes sticky wages and flexible prices, consumption and labor are not particularly pro-cyclical (even less than the data suggest), implying that a major weakness of RBC models has been mitigated.

3.5 Some notes on monetary policy

In this section, we more closely investigate the role of monetary policy in our model. Figure 3.4 in appendix 3.C shows the economic aggregate IRFs in response to a 1% shock to the interest rate. As expected, all key variables react negatively to this monetary contraction. However, the impact of the monetary shock is relatively low in absolute terms based on the deviation of the other variables. While this especially holds for weighted average productivity, this result is not surprising. An increase in the interest rate has two main effects. First, it raises the cost of market entry, resulting in fewer producing firms and, due to less competition, lower cut-off productivity (partially as a result of lower TFP). Second, lower demand and increasing fixed production costs result in an increase in cut-off productivity (and therefore of $\tilde{\varphi}_t$).[69] As one can see from the respective IRF, the first effect narrowly dominates after the shock according to our calibration.

To better understand the role of monetary policy, we compare the impact of a change in Taylor rule parameters on the IRFs of the most important economic aggregates (weighted average productivity, output, number of firms, consumption). The baseline scenario is the same as in section 3.4.2, i.e., we simulate a 1% shock

[69]cp. equation (3.16).

to the minimum productivity level, φ_t^{min}, and use the same calibration applied in table 3.1. We then repeat the simulation by varying the monetary policy weight on output, θ_y. We keep θ_π, the weight on inflation, constant because price inflation varies only marginally. Figure 3.3 shows the respective IRFs for three alternative scenarios. In one scenario, the central bank gives less weight to output variation, i.e., θ_y is set to a fourth of its estimated value. In the other two scenarios, the monetary authority attaches more weight to stabilizing output, i.e., θ_y is increased by three- and five-fold, respectively.

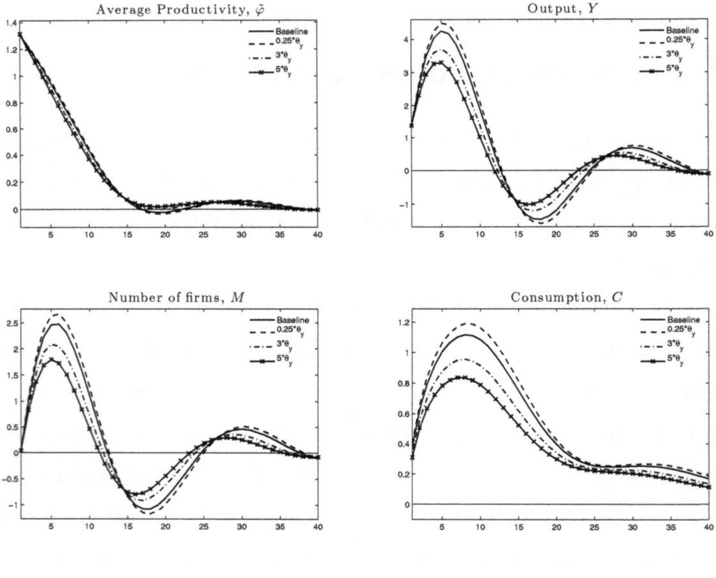

Figure 3.3: Impulse response functions for different Taylor rule parameters.

The results show that monetary policy effectively stabilizes the economy, and this finding holds for all aggregates. In particular, with respect to output, the number of firms and consumption, we can observe pronounced differences between the generated IRFs and several monetary policy rules. For example, the variation in output decreases by more than one fourth relative to the baseline calibration when the weighting parameter, θ_y, is multiplied by three. This strong impact is not surprising, as monetary policy influences not only the demand side but also the number of producing firms.

The weighted average productivity indeed reacts to alternative monetary policy parameters, although in a significantly less pronounced manner due to the mechanism described above, i.e., a more pronounced central bank reaction increases the effective fixed cost of production and, together with lower demand, results in a rise in cut-off productivity, φ_t^*, and therefore in TFP. On the contrary, less competition leads to a consequent decrease in the cut-off and, thus, the weighted average productivity level. Overall, we find that monetary policy does have a stabilizing effect on TFP. This result may be an additional factor for the monetary authority, e.g., when we assume a "learning-by-doing-effect", i.e., that weighted average productivity has a positive feedback effect on technology determinants as, for example, the steady state minimum productivity level, $\overline{\varphi}^{min}$ (or its growth rate).[70] In such cases, excessive (or insufficient) stabilization can negatively affect the long-term development of the economy, which must be considered by the central bank when developing its monetary policy.

3.6 Conclusion

Motivated by the empirically documented importance of net business formation for business cycles, we have developed a new Keynesian model that includes endogenous firm entry/exit, heterogeneous productivity across firms, and sticky wages but flexible prices. The model depicts a new amplification mechanism of exogenous productivity shocks. The entrance of new firms following a positive shock (due to lower entry costs and higher expected profits) leads to more competition, i.e., incumbent firms must be relatively more productive to make positive profits

[70]See, for example, Blackburn (1999) for a similar approach to a monetary model.

and thus stay in the market, leading to higher average productivity within the economy. This in turn renders market entry less attractive. When the first effect dominates, we observe an acceleration effect. The quantitative results suggest that approximately 56% of the variation in TFP can be attributed to this interaction.

Regarding the second-moment properties of the key economic variables, our model largely outperforms comparable models that include endogenous entry and reports variances in output, consumption and investment that are remarkably close to the data. The described amplification mechanism plays a central role in allowing the model to reproduce these patterns. Finally, regarding the influence of monetary policy, we can observe a stabilizing impact on all economic aggregates including, although only to a small extent, economy-wide weighted average productivity. Nevertheless, assuming a "learning-by-doing-effect", this impact on weighted average productivity may play a role in optimal monetary policy.

There are many possible directions for future research. From a theoretical perspective, an extension of our model would explicitly consider the feedback effect of TFP in a growth environment. There may also be implications for fiscal policy (most likely in interaction with monetary policy).[71] Nevertheless, the role of net business formation and product creation must be considered in further empirical research. This is especially true regarding interactions between productivity and monetary policy. Detailed firm-level data containing information on costs and product creation should be included in such an analysis.

[71] See Chugh and Ghironi (2011) for an analysis of fiscal policy in a Bilbiie et al. (2012) framework.

Appendix

3.A Linearized model

The following system of equations describes the linearized version of the model. Hatted variables denote percentage deviations from the steady state, and variables without a time subscript denote steady state values. To simplify the calculations, we introduce a new variable in the linearized version, $p_t^{in} := 1 - G_t(\varphi_t^*)$, which denotes the probability of entering the market after drawing a new productivity level, φ. Using the parametrization from section 3.3.9, this implies that $p_t^{in} = \left(\frac{\varphi_t^{min}}{\varphi_t^*}\right)^{\kappa}$.

$$\frac{1}{1-h}\left(\hat{c}_t - h\hat{c}_{t\;1}\right) = \frac{1}{1-h}\left(\hat{c}_{t+1} - h\hat{c}_t\right) + \hat{\pi}_{t+1} - \frac{i}{1+i}\hat{i}_t \qquad \text{(Euler equation)}$$

$$\frac{i}{1+i}\hat{i}_{t+1} - \hat{\pi}_{t+1} = \frac{q}{(1-\delta)+q}\left(\hat{q}_{t+1}\right) \qquad \text{(Capital accumulation)}$$

$$\hat{w}_t - \hat{w}_{t\;1} = \beta E_t[\hat{w}_{t+1} - \hat{w}_t]$$
$$-\lambda^w\left(\hat{w}_t - \hat{\Upsilon}_t + \hat{\tilde{\varphi}}_t + \frac{1-\rho}{\rho}\hat{m}_t - \eta\hat{l}_t - \frac{1}{1-h}\left(\hat{c}_t - h\hat{c}_{t\;1}\right) - \frac{i}{1+i}\hat{i}_t\right)$$
$$\text{(Wage setting)}$$

$$\hat{\Gamma}_{t+1} = \alpha\hat{k}_t + (1-\alpha)\hat{l}_t \qquad \text{(Input good production)}$$

$$\hat{\Upsilon}_t = \alpha^2\hat{q}_t + \alpha(1-\alpha)\hat{w}_t + (1-\alpha)\left(\hat{\tilde{\varphi}}_t + \frac{1-\rho}{\rho}\hat{m}_t\right) \qquad \text{(Price of input good)}$$

$$\hat{q}_t = (1-\alpha)(\hat{l}_t - \hat{k}_t) \qquad \text{(Rental rate of capital)}$$

$$\hat{\pi}_t = (\hat{\Upsilon}_t - \hat{\Upsilon}_{t\ 1}) - \frac{1-\rho}{\rho}(\hat{m}_t - \hat{m}_{t\ 1}) - (\hat{\tilde{\varphi}}_t - \hat{\tilde{\varphi}}_{t\ 1}) \qquad \text{(Inflation)}$$

$$\hat{\varphi}^*_t = \frac{1-\rho}{\rho}\left[\frac{i}{1+i}\hat{i}_t + \frac{1}{\rho}\hat{m}_t + \frac{1}{1-\rho}\hat{\tilde{\varphi}}_t - \hat{y}_t\right] \qquad \text{(Zero cut-off condition)}$$

$$\widehat{p^{in}}_t = \kappa\left(\hat{\varphi}^{min}_t - \hat{\varphi}^*_t\right) \qquad \text{(Probability of entering)}$$

$$\hat{\varphi}^{min}_t = \zeta\hat{\varphi}^{min}_{t\ 1} + \log(\varepsilon_t) \qquad \text{(Minimum productivity level)}$$

$$\hat{\tilde{\varphi}}_t = \hat{\varphi}^*_t \qquad \text{(Weighted average productivity)}$$

$$\frac{(1-\rho)Y}{1+i}\left(\hat{y}_t - \frac{i}{1+i}\hat{i}_t\right) - fM^{1/\rho}\tilde{\varphi}\rho\left(\frac{1}{\rho}\hat{m}_t + \hat{\tilde{\varphi}}_t\right) = \frac{f_e M}{p^{in}}\left(\hat{m}_t - \widehat{p^{in}}_t\right)$$

(Free entry condition)

$$Y\hat{y}_t = M^{\frac{1-\rho}{\rho}}\tilde{\varphi}\Gamma\left(\frac{1-\rho}{\rho}\hat{m}_t + \hat{\tilde{\varphi}}_t + \hat{\Gamma}_t\right)$$

$$-M^{1/\rho}\tilde{\varphi}f\left(\frac{1}{\rho}\hat{m}_t + \hat{\tilde{\varphi}}_t\right) - \frac{Mf_e}{p^{in}}\left(\hat{m}_t - \widehat{p^{in}}_t\right) \qquad \text{(Total production)}$$

$$C\hat{c}_t = Y\hat{y}_t - K\left(\hat{k}_{t+1} - (1-\delta)\hat{k}_t\right) \qquad \text{(Household consumption)}$$

$$\hat{i}_t = \xi\hat{i}_{t\ 1} + (1-\xi)\left[\theta_y\hat{y}_t + \theta_\pi\hat{\pi}_t\right] \qquad \text{(Taylor rule)}$$

3.B OLS-regression for the Taylor rule

To calibrate the Taylor rule parameters, we perform an OLS-regression for the 1984Q1-2013Q3 period for the mean deviation of the federal fund rate on its own lag, the mean deviation of real GDP growth, and the mean deviation of the quarterly consumer price inflation rate. Data on the federal fund rate and CPI are provided by the Federal Reserve, and data on real GDP are drawn from the US Bureau of Economic Analysis. Table 3.3 shows the results of the estimation. Estimated coefficients are used to calibrate the Taylor rule parameters in the structural model.

Table 3.3: Estimation of Taylor rule parameters.

Dep. var.: *Fed. fund rate (deviation from mean)*	
Fed. fund rate (deviation from mean)$_{t-1}$	0.859***
	(0.076)
Real GDP growth (deviation from mean)	0.048**
	(0.024)
Inflation (deviation from mean)	0.057**
	(0.023)
Constant	−0.017
	(0.028)
Adjusted R^2	0.806
Period	1984Q1-2013Q3

Robust standard errors in parentheses

* $p < 0.1$, ** $p < 0.05$, *** $p < 0.01$

3.C Impulse response functions following a monetary shock

Figure 3.4 shows key aggregate reactions to a monetary shock by percentage deviation from the zero-inflation steady state.

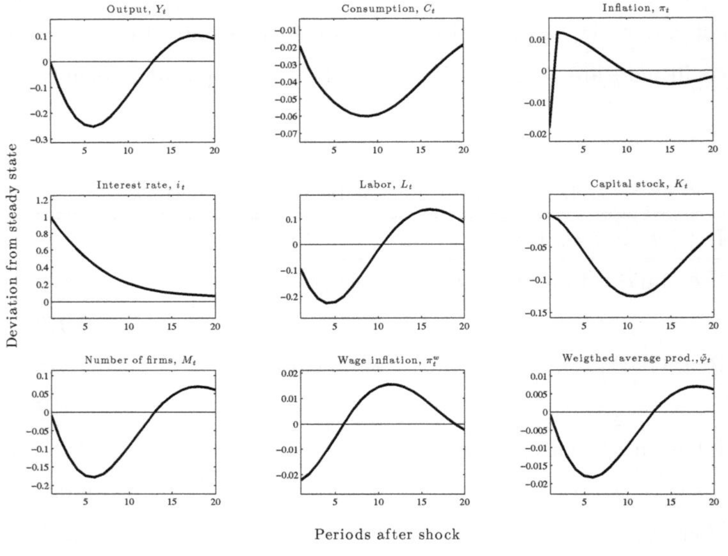

Figure 3.4: Impulse response functions II.
Percentage deviation from the steady state for key variables following a positive, 1% shock to the nominal interest rate. Periods refer to quarters.

4 What Determines Price Changes and the Distribution of Prices? Evidence from the Swiss CPI.***

joint with Reto Föllmi and Rudolf Minsch

Abstract

This chapter examines how firms set and adjust their prices, depending on macroeconomic, sectoral and individual conditions. A large panel of 345,963 observations of quarterly firm and product price data, underlying the Swiss sectoral CPIs from 1993 to 2012, is used for this purpose. The data allows us to trace the pricing decisions of the identified firm over time and in detail (without regular interruption of the price series as in the case of the US CPI). Among several macroeconomic factors, the appreciation of the Swiss franc results in an increase in the probability of a positive price change and, to a lesser extent, in the size of price changes. Singling out one policy measure, we found that an increase in the VAT is overproportionally shifted to prices by firms who change their prices. Finally, the data set allows for the analysis of the development of price dispersion at the product

***The authors thank Martin Huber and Lukas Schmid, as well as the participants of the April 3, 2014, Sinergia-Seminar at the University of Zurich, and the participants of the 2014 conference of the Swiss Society of Economics and Statistics in Bern for their helpful comments and suggestions. We are also very grateful to Hans-Markus Herren from the Swiss Federal Statistical Office, who provided us with the data. The usual disclaimer applies.

level. We can demonstrate that an increase in the VAT led to a decrease in the variance in prices, whereas macroeconomic factors have no impact.

Keywords: Price Setting Behavior of Firms, Frequency of Price Changes, Price Dispersion
JEL-Classification: E31, E37, E52

4.1 Introduction

The price setting behavior of firms is central to understanding macroeconomic policies. Price stickiness is well documented in the empirical literature (e.g., Bils and Klenow (2004), Álvarez et al. (2006)). However, most papers focus on the frequency of price adjustments, i.e., the extensive margin, without studying the sizes of price changes. In contrast, there is little available knowledge on the intensive margin, i.e., the extent to which a firm adjusts its prices and what determines the size of a price change. The same lack of knowledge is true for price setting vis-à-vis competitors, i.e., for the distribution of prices over time.

This chapter attempts to fill these two gaps by using a panel data set of specific product prices underlying several Swiss sectoral CPI data series. The sectors are typical non-tradable services, i.e., cinemas, hairdressers and restaurants (food and drinks). The advantage of this data set is that it allows an apportionment of each data point to a specific firm, sector or product group, and does not rely on a qualitative survey. A unique feature compared to other datasets is that the price series of individual firms do not interrupt on a regular basis as this is the case, for example, for US CPI data.[72] This enables us to estimate the average level and the dispersion of the entire price distribution. Consequently, we can look at many theoretically relevant state-dependent factors for pricing decision as well, in particular the relative position of the firm's price to the average price in the market.

We investigate the observable factors that influence price setting behavior at both the extensive and intensive margins, i.e., the frequency and the (average) size of price changes. Following the literature, we distinguish between time-dependent and state-dependent variables, while a particular focus lay in the impact of the macroeconomic environment. In agreement with previous results (see the following section), we find that time-dependent variables are of less importance, with the

[72]cp. Klenow and Kryvtsov (2008).

exception of seasonality components, i.e., we can observe not only more but also, on average, stronger price adjustments during the first quarter of a year. State-dependent factors are of greater importance. The position of the firm's price relative to the average of its competitors is particularly relevant. We find that not only the probability but also the size of a price change increase to a greater extent the further a price is from the average price of the product.

Among several policy parameters, we study the impact of changes in the value-added tax (VAT), addressing how this external cost shock or its anticipation are reflected in prices. During the observed period, Switzerland experienced four increases in the VAT. Changes in the VAT, compared to other tax changes or policy measures, are particularly applicable to study because they can be considered as completely exogenous because Switzerland does not use this tax as an instrument of economic policy. Our results indicate that firms who change their prices raise their prices more than the VAT increase, controlling for other factors, while the firms' costs increase only proportionally with the rise in the VAT. Thus, firms appear to regard a change in the VAT as an opportunity to increase their markups.

Finally, the phenomenon of price dispersion is gaining interest in macroeconomics as producer heterogeneity has become increasingly important. Our results indicate that an increase in the VAT led to a decrease in the variance in prices. This may stem therefrom that firms with a low price, relative to their competitors, adjust their prices upward when the VAT increases. Macroeconomic factors, however, do not appear to play a role, whereas other moments (i.e., skewness and kurtosis) are not influenced by the VAT.

The remainder of the paper is organized as follows. Section 4.2 provides a review of the relevant literature. Section 4.3 describes the data and provides descriptive statistics. Section 4.4 presents the results of the econometric estimations regarding the price setting behavior, whereas section 4.5 reports on the analysis of the development of price dispersion. Finally, section 4.6 concludes the chapter.

4.2 Review of related literature

There are several theoretical models explaining the (not perfectly flexible) price setting behavior of firms from a macroeconomic perspective. Two branches can be identified. On the one hand, *time-dependent* models consider the timing of price changes as exogenously given, meaning that only the size of the price change is chosen by the respective firm. The most cited and widely employed approach has been developed by Calvo (1983) and implies that a specific firm can adjust its price in each period with a given, constant probability. A similar earlier model, developed by Taylor (1980), considers the length of contracts as fixed and postulates that prices can only be changed at the beginning of a contract.[73] Other models, such as the sticky information approach developed by Mankiw and Reis (2002), retains the central hypothesis of time-dependent price setting behavior by firms. On the other hand, *state-dependent* pricing, generally referred to as menu cost models, assumes that firms react to idiosyncratic shocks, i.e., that firms' pricing decisions are made independent of timing (Dotsey et al., 1999; Gertler and Leahy, 2008; Golosov and Lucas, 2007). A popular approach following this view is proposed by Rotemberg (1982), who models price changes as costly actions while costs increase disproportionally with the sizes of price changes. A newer approach following the same main idea is the rational inattention model developed by Maćkowiak and Wiederholt (2009), which assumes that firms decide what to pay attention to, which is a constrained action. Thus, firms cannot adjust prices fully flexibly, because they do not consistently possess all the necessary information.

Most empirical research focuses on the frequency of price adjustments and their determinants and devotes less attention to the sizes of price changes. On the one hand, this lack of attention is a direct consequence of most theoretical models also tending to concentrate on frequency (as a measure of price stickiness). On the other hand, this lack might also be the result of limited data availability. Cecchetti

[73] See also Taylor (1979) for the case of wage contracts.

(1986) uses data on the newsstand prices of American magazines to find a relationship between inflation and the frequency of price adjustments, a finding that is also supported by other authors. However, Cecchetti (1986) only concentrates on a single product. A broader set of data, i.e., twelve selected retail goods, is therefore considered by Kashyap (1995), who states that prices are normally fixed for more than one year; however, he also clearly emphasizes that the time between price changes is irregular, i.e., there is likely no stable frequency. It is therefore unsurprising that other papers report different frequencies. Bils and Klenow (2004), for example, who considers more than 350 categories of consumer goods, examines a frequency of approximately five months. Nakamura and Steinsson (2008) propose that 9-12% of prices change every month, but the price adjustments are highly seasonal, i.e., most prices change at the beginning of a year.

There is a small literature concerned with state-dependent pricing. Lein (2010) uses a survey across industrial firms in Switzerland where state-dependent variables are empirically important. Her data set also allows her to consider the impact of individual cost structures and expectations but not the sizes of price changes. Kaufmann (2009) considers a very similar data set to ours and for a broader set of subindices; however, his contribution remains descriptive. Honoré et al. (2012) also use data from subindices of the Swiss CPI to investigate the contribution of general inflation to the share of positive price changes in Switzerland.[74]

As mentioned above, little is empirically understood about the factors impacting the sizes of price adjustments. An exemption is the seminal work of Klenow and Kryvtsov (2008). These authors use item-based pricing for three sub-areas of the US CPI, suggesting that the frequency and size of price adjustments are unrelated to the timing. However, they do not discuss the size of the impact of macroeconomic fluctuations or developments. Our Swiss CPI data allow to

[74]Certain studies investigate the reaction of sectoral price indices (instead of prices in a narrow sense) to macroeconomic disturbances, e.g., Boivin et al. (2009), Maćkowiak et al. (2009), Kaufmann and Lein (2013), and Altissimo et al. (2009).

estimate with reasonable precision the average and the dispersion of prices in a sector, since firms stay for a long time in our sample. This allows us to consider a broader set of state-dependent variables such as the relative price level of a firm vis-à-vis its competitors. In addition and again different to Klenow and Kryvtsov (2008),we study the pricing impact of macroeconomic fluctuations as well.

Regarding price dispersion, the existing empirical literature only focuses on very small industries, brief periods, or price dispersion across countries. Borenstein and Rose (1994), for example, examine the airline industry in 1986 and found greater dispersion on routes with more competition.[75] Sorensen (2000) analyzes the distribution of prices charged by different pharmacies for several drugs. Clay et al. (2001) investigate the effects of advertising and branding on the differentiation of prices between online bookstores, and they observe a positive impact. Kaplan and Menzio (2014) follow a more general approach and investigate the shape and structure of the distribution of prices at which an identical good is sold. They find that the typical price distribution is symmetric. However, an earlier work by Lach and Tsiddon (1992) on the prices of food in Israel indicates that, with higher inflation, the price distribution of a given product becomes more right skewed.

A comparison of the general price levels among EMU countries is performed by Hoeberichts and Stokman (2011), finding that the dispersion of price levels is negatively related to business cycles. Contrary to existing work, our data set allows us to observe price dispersions for many products over a relatively long period.

[75]Sengupta and Wiggins (2014) extend this line of analysis by accounting for online purchases of airline fares. They do not observe reduced dispersion following increased online shopping.

4.3 Data description and descriptive statistics

4.3.1 The data

Our analysis is based on a set of panel data on the underlying subindices of the Swiss CPI. The data are provided by the Swiss Federal Office of Statistics (SFOS). The data set allows us to track the development of a single price for a given product charged by a given firm over time. Data are available for four subindices of the Swiss CPI: hairdressers, cinemas, food in restaurants, and drinks in restaurants, representing a total weight of 4.13% in the Swiss CPI in 2013. These four available sectors all represent classical non-tradable services.[76]

The data appear on a quarterly basis from 1993Q2 to 2012Q4. Firms and products enter and exit the data set on an irregular basis, but these changes are documented.[77] Thus, a few prices can be tracked over the entire sample, which is a central advantage of the data set over others (e.g., Klenow and Kryvtsov (2008), in which products always drop out the data set after at most five years). Furthermore, only 0.21% of all the recorded price changes in the data set are due to temporary sales, which largely eliminate a critical source of disturbances in the estimation. A disadvantage of the data is that we could not observe any additional information about the tracked firms, i.e., we do not know anything about the location or size.

In the second quarter of 2000, we observe a disproportionately large number of firms and products that are replaced, because the method for calculating the CPI in Switzerland changed at this point in time.[78] A limited number of substantial price jumps indicate potential measurement errors at this time; however, we retain these observations in the data because they have little impact on the results.

The data set records, based on the statistical criteria of the SFOS, whether a

[76]Note that detailed price data underlying the Swiss CPI are normally confidential and unavailable, which is why data on additional sectors are not available.

[77]Further, the total number of recorded prices varies over time. On average, a firm remains for 35.33 periods and a single product for 21.74 periods in the sample.

[78]See Kaufmann (2009) for a broader discussion.

certain product is replaced by a new one, e.g., because of a substantial quality improvement. If we observe such a replacement, we consider the given price series as terminated and begin a new one. Using this procedure, we have a total of 15,932 price series consisting of 73 different products. Overall, the data comprises 345,963 observations representing an unbalanced panel structure.

Table 4.1 provides an overview of the data structure. Note that the total number of observations refers to the number of observed prices and not to the number of price changes.

Table 4.1: Overview data.

Specification	**Number**
Producers (or firms), j	457
Product groups, Ω	4
Products, i	73
Price series, $p(i_n, j)$	15,932
Quarters, t	79
Observations, $p(i_n, j, t)$	345,963
Time span	1993Q2-2012Q4

4.3.2 Constructed variables

Three variables are constructed from the data. The first reflects, at each point in time and for each price series, the number of periods since the last non-zero price change. Let $p(i_n, j, t)$ be the price of product i_n (where n is the number of the product, if the same product type, i, is sold more than once by the same firm), charged by firm j in period t; then, $\hat{p}(i_n, j, t) := \frac{p(i_n,j,t)\quad p(i_n,j,t\quad 1)}{p(i_n,j,t\quad 1)}$ subsequently defines the respective relative change in this price. Furthermore, we denote $k_1(i_n, j), k_2(i_n, j), \ldots, k_m(i_n, j), \ldots, k_M(i_n, j)$ as those periods during which we observe a change in the price, $p(i_n, j, t)$. In formal terms:

$$t = \begin{cases} k_m(i_n, j), & \text{if } \hat{p}(i_n, j, t) \neq 0 \\ k_m(i_n, j) + z(i_n, j, t), & \text{otherwise} \end{cases}, \tag{4.1}$$

where $z(i_n, j, t,) := \min_{k_m(i_n,j)<t} (t - k_m(i_n, j)) \,\forall\, t, m$ therefore represents the desired number of periods since the last price change. In constructing the variable $z(i_n, j, t,)$, we were forced to omit the data before the first price change in every price series, i.e., all data points at $t < k_1(i_n, j)$. This procedure follows Klenow and Kryvtsov (2008), who also note that the estimations would be biased otherwise.

Second, we are interested in the accumulated sectoral inflation after a price change as a measurement of the general development of prices. Each product, i, belongs to one of the four Swiss CPI subindices considered, which we denote as Ω.[79] $\text{CPI}_{\Omega(i)}(t)$ therefore represents the subindex to which product i belongs (in period t). Given this notation, the inflation accumulated since the last price change, denoted $\pi(i_n, j, t)$, is defined as follows:

$$\pi(i_n, j, t) := \min_{k_m(i_n,j)<t} \frac{\text{CPI}_{\Omega(i)}(t-1) - \text{CPI}_{\Omega(i)}(k_m(i_n, j))}{\text{CPI}_{\Omega(i)}(k_m(i_n, j))}. \tag{4.2}$$

Note that equation (4.2) implies that accumulated inflation is measured as the inflation occurring between the last price change and period $t-1$, which is assumed for the following reason: A firm that is deciding whether it wishes to change one of its prices in period t only knows the inflation rate prior to period $t-1$, because the inflation rate of period t remains unknown until all the firms have made their pricing decisions in period t. Moreover, the construction of the variable also prevents a potential endogeneity problem.

Third and as a particular feature of our dataset, we are able to calculate each price relative to the mean price of its product category, i, at each point in time, t. For this purpose, we define $A(i, t) := \sum_{n,j} 1_t[p(i_n, j, t)]$ as the total (unweighted)

[79]Data on the Swiss CPI subindices are provided by the SFOS.

number of observed prices of product i in period t. Thus, $1_t[.]$ is an indicator function taking a value equal to one if $p(i_n, j, t) > 0$ in period t and zero otherwise. Denoting the individual deviation from the mean price as $\rho(i_n, j, t)$, we can define

$$\rho(i_n, j, t) := \frac{p(i_n, j, t)}{\frac{1}{A(i,t)} \sum_{n,j} p(i_n, j, t)} - 1. \tag{4.3}$$

Note that, by construction, it holds that $\frac{1}{A(i,t)} \sum_{n,j} \rho(i_n, j, t) = 0 \; \forall \, i, t$. The variable $\rho(i_n, j, t)$ provides us with a measurement of the competitive standing of the respective price. It is clear that this measurement is only an approximation, because we cannot observe other important factors, such as distance to the nearest competitor or other cost factors.

4.3.3 Descriptive statistics

Table 4.2 presents the frequency of price changes (positive and negative) disaggregated by each individual product sector, Ω. In the full sample, the prices are changed in 9% of all the observations. Compared to the literature, the firms in our data set change prices relatively infrequently. Lein (2010), for example, report values for Swiss manufacturers that are three times higher. The reason for this difference may lie in the different set of products (non-tradable services) that our data set contains.

Table 4.2: Share of price changes.

Product sector, Ω	Cinema	Hairdresser	Rest., drinks	Rest., food	**Total**
Price change (abs.)	6.0%	8.9%	9.4%	9.1%	**9.1%**
Pos. price change	5.1%	8.4%	8.2%	7.4%	**7.8%**
Neg. price change	0.9%	0.5%	1.2%	1.7%	**1.3%**
Numb. of observations	12,870	42,104	132,140	142,893	**330,007**
Numb. of firms in total	67	198	189	188	**457**

The data also suggest strong downward price rigidity, in line with the findings provided by Kaufmann (2009), which can to some extent be explained by the nominal downward rigidity of wages, as described by Fehr and Goette (2005) for the case of Switzerland.

Figure 4.1 graphically illustrates the (unweighted) frequency of price changes over time, measured as a share of all the observations in each quarter. The graph provides two main insights. First, the peaks in the first quarters of 1995 and 1999 and, to a lesser extent, in the first quarters of 2001 and 2012 reflect the increases in the VAT that occurred at these times. In the first quarter of 1995, when the VAT was introduced, 75.5% of all of the prices in the sample were changed.[80] Second, the graph indicates that the frequency of price changes is seasonal, with a peak in the first quarter of the year and a decrease thereafter.

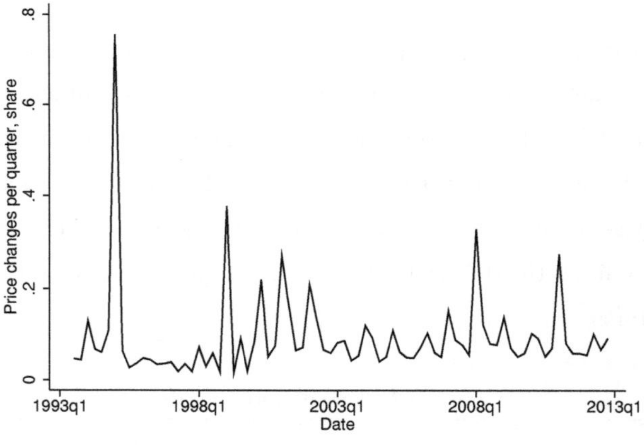

Figure 4.1: Frequency of price changes, on a quarterly basis.
Notes: Price changes related to sales are excluded.

The seasonality of the frequency of price changes is also supported when examin-

[80]Note that the service sector in Switzerland was not required to pay any sales or value-added taxes before this point in time.

ing the distribution of time periods between price changes, $z(i_n, j, t,)$, as illustrated in figure 4.2. As with most models, the distribution is right skewed, i.e., the more time that has passed since the last price change, the greater the probability is that a firm will adjust its prices. However, we can also observe a local peak in every fourth period, indicating the above-mentioned concentration of price changes during the first quarter of the year.

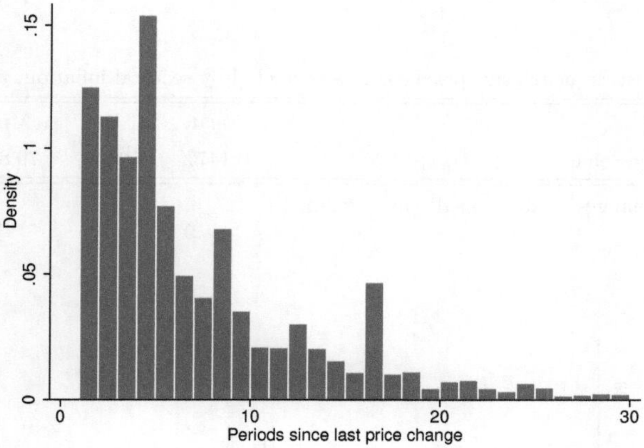

Figure 4.2: Distribution of times between price changes, $z(i_n, j, t,)$.
Notes: Price changes related to sales are excluded.

Contrary to many other datasets, we are able to calculate not only the frequency but also the size of price changes. Table 4.3 and figure 4.3 describe how the size of non-zero price changes are distributed. For this purpose, we normalize the data in the sense that we subtract the accumulated sectoral inflation at every non-zero price change (data points without a price change, constituting the majority, are excluded), i.e., the statistics refer to data of the following form:

$$\hat{p}_{norm}(i_n, j, t) := \begin{cases} \hat{p}(i_n, j, t) - \pi(i_n, j, t), & \text{if } \hat{p}(i_n, j, t) \neq 0 \\ \emptyset, & \text{otherwise} \end{cases}. \tag{4.4}$$

The normalization allows us to interpret the size of a price change while abstracting from the potential "distortion" of the general price development. Consequently, the average normalized price change is therefore not statistically different from zero. We can observe a relatively broad distribution of price changes, implying that other factors might also be important in the price setting process. However, the distribution is right skewed, providing some evidence for the potential real downward rigidity of price setting.

Table 4.3: Statistics for relative price changes corrected by sectoral inflation, $\hat{p}_{norm}(i_n, j, t)$.

	Mean	St.Dev.	Min.	Max.
Normalized price change, $\hat{p}_{norm}(i_n, j, t)$	0.147%	2.243%	-79.86%	193.2%

Notes: Price changes related to sales are excluded.

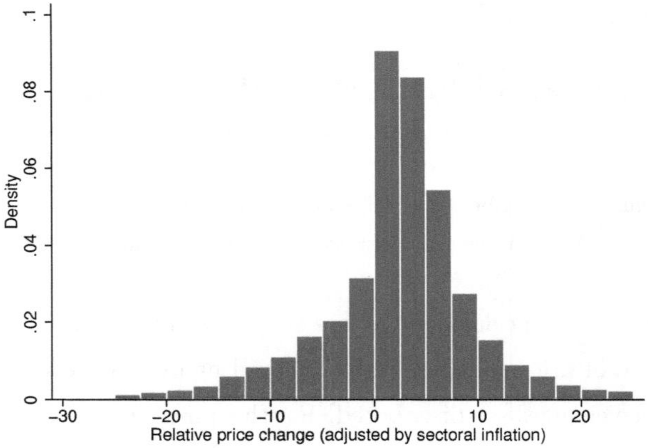

Figure 4.3: Histogram of relative price changes corrected by sectoral inflation, $\hat{p}_{norm}(i_n, j, t)$.
Notes: Price changes related to sales are excluded.

4.4 Econometric results

4.4.1 Methodology

Two types of estimations are conducted in this section. First, we focus on the extensive margin, i.e., we estimate how the different factors influence the probability of a (positive or negative) price change. A conditional logit model is employed for this purpose. The conditional form is appropriate because we are unable to observe any individual attributes of firms or price series within the data set. In the second part, we focus on the intensive margin, i.e., we estimate how the various factors influence the sizes of price adjustments on average (i.e., we also consider the data points with no price changes because these represent also pricing decisions) by relying on a standard OLS framework.

In each of the two models, we estimate three regression specifications, but the specifications differ in the numbers of variables included. The first specification is estimated by using only time-dependent variables and the variables concerning the VAT, as a specific and important policy measure.[81] The time-dependent variables consist of the number of periods between two price changes, $z(i_n, j, t)$, as well as dummies for the first, second and third quarters of each year.

The variables concerning the VAT are of three types. One reports the relative change in the VAT in the quarter when this change occurs.[82] The second group of VAT variables simply consists of the first two lags of the first variable. The third type of variable consists of the relative change in the VAT at the points in time when this change is officially known to occur in some number of quarters in the future and is zero otherwise. For the case of Switzerland, this condition means that a change in the VAT is approved through a popular vote or the deadline for a referendum against an increase in the VAT has passed. The VAT increases in

[81]See also Kaufmann (2009) who observe a significant impact of of the VAT at the aggregated level.

[82]The relative change in the VAT, denoted τ_t (for period t), is determined as follows: $\frac{1+\tau_t}{1+\tau_{t-1}} - 1$.

1995 and 2001 were therefore known four quarters before they were enacted. The VAT increases in 1999 and 2012 were known three and five quarters in advance, respectively.

The second specification adds the accumulated sectoral inflation, $\pi(i_n, j, t)$, and the relative deviation from the mean price, $\rho(i_n, j, t-1)$, as proxies for price-series-specific state variables.[83] Finally, the third specification includes variables for the macroeconomic environment. These variables are real year-on-year GDP growth, the quarter-on-quarter growth rate of the real exchange rate index, and the first difference in the three-month LIBOR interest rate.[84] All the macroeconomic variables add up to a lag of four quarters.[85]

A dummy for the second quarter of 2000 is also included in each estimation, and the same holds for starting and ending points of temporary sales.[86] All the estimations also include product-series-specific fixed effects to control for series-specific shocks. Because the firm is the relevant pricing decision unit, standard errors are clustered at the firm level, as proposed by Lein (2010).

4.4.2 Pricing at the extensive margin

This section analyzes the factors that influence individual pricing decisions at the extensive margin (i.e., whether a firm changes its price), using a conditional logit probability model. The estimations for the three specifications are performed

[83]To capture the effect on the actual pricing decision, the latter is measured in the pre-period.

[84]Data on the real GDP growth are provided by the SFOS. Data on the real exchange rate index and the LIBOR are provided by the Swiss National Bank. Note that the use of the exchange rate relative to the euro, instead of the real exchange rate index, affects the results only slightly.

[85]One might argue that future expectations of these variables might also play roles. However, the use of lags can be considered a reduced form, because expectations are also functions of past realizations.

[86]The dummy for the second quarter of 2000 is included because of the relatively high proportion of product replacements during this period due to a change in the method for calculating the CPI. See section 4.3.1.

twice: once for positive price changes and once for negative price changes. All the tables report marginal effects evaluated at the variables' means, given no price-series-specific shocks. For the dummy variables, the marginal effects are calculated at the change of the dummy from 0 to 1.

Table 4.4 presents the results of the estimations, which are generally in line with the literature regarding the role of the number of periods since the last price change and the confirmation of the descriptive evidence that most price changes occur in the first quarter of a year, i.e., seasonality is the most important time-dependent factor. The respective coefficient is highly significant in all estimations and specifications.

Table 4.4: Cond. logit probability model.

Panel A: Positive price changes	Specification 1	Specification 2	Specification 3
Rel. change VAT	0.709***	0.737***	0.611***
	(0.047)	(0.055)	(0.055)
Rel.chan. VAT, 1 Lag(s)	0.037	0.004	0.069
	(0.055)	(0.052)	(0.056)
Rel.chan. VAT, 2 Lag(s)	0.017	0.010	0.092
	(0.058)	(0.058)	(0.064)
Fut.VAT-incr. known, 1 Lag(s)	0.249***	0.244***	0.234***
	(0.053)	(0.051)	(0.057)
Fut.VAT-incr. known, 2 Lag(s)	0.180***	0.177***	0.235***
	(0.061)	(0.060)	(0.058)
Fut.VAT-incr. known, 3 Lag(s)	0.068	0.055	0.093
	(0.106)	(0.092)	(0.070)
Fut.VAT-incr. known, 4 Lag(s)	0.004	0.024	0.040
	(0.070)	(0.072)	(0.063)
Fut.VAT-incr. known, 5 Lag(s)	0.158	0.035	0.220
	(0.603)	(0.601)	(1.054)
Periods since last price change, $z(i_n, j, t,)$	0.125***	0.091***	0.081***
	(0.011)	(0.014)	(0.014)
$z(i_n, j, t,)^2$	0.001***	0.002***	0.002***
	(0.000)	(0.000)	(0.000)
Dummy 1st quarter	1.285***	1.330***	1.304***
	(0.093)	(0.093)	(0.108)
Dummy 2nd quarter	0.596***	0.573***	0.580***
	(0.100)	(0.099)	(0.117)
Dummy 3rd quarter	0.111	0.099	0.229**
	(0.086)	(0.086)	(0.094)

Sales	14.623***	13.892***	13.718***
	(0.493)	(0.526)	(0.467)
Sales end	3.225***	2.770***	2.865***
	(0.536)	(0.484)	(0.458)
Dummy 2000Q2	0.871***	1.052***	1.246***
	(0.148)	(0.154)	(0.200)
Acc.sec.infl., $\pi(i_n, j, t)$		0.096***	0.140***
		(0.035)	(0.036)
Price relative to mean price, $\rho(i_n, j, t \quad 1)$		0.072***	0.073***
		(0.005)	(0.005)
$\rho(i_n, j, t \quad 1)^2$		0.001**	0.001**
		(0.000)	(0.000)
GDP growth, yoy			0.028
			(0.042)
Lag 1 quarters			0.028
			(0.067)
Lag 2 quarters			0.006
			(0.068)
Lag 3 quarters			0.150**
			(0.064)
Lag 4 quarters			0.255***
			(0.037)
RER index, gr. qoq			0.099***
			(0.015)
Lag 1 quarters			0.101***
			(0.019)
Lag 2 quarters			0.014
			(0.019)
Lag 3 quarters			0.044***
			(0.017)
Lag 4 quarters			0.025
			(0.018)
3m LIBOR, 1st diff.			0.069
			(0.106)
Lag 1 quarters			0.098
			(0.110)
Lag 2 quarters			0.382***
			(0.096)
Lag 3 quarters			0.082
			(0.126)
Lag 4 quarters			0.136
			(0.095)
Pseudo R^2	0.162	0.186	0.208
Observations	180,032	180,032	180,032

Panel B: Negative price changes	Specification 1	Specification 2	Specification 3
Rel. change VAT	0.032	0.091*	0.142**
	(0.047)	(0.047)	(0.062)
Rel.chan. VAT, 1 Lag(s)	0.223***	0.265***	0.299***
	(0.068)	(0.072)	(0.076)
Rel.chan. VAT, 2 Lag(s)	0.093	0.135**	0.174***
	(0.058)	(0.058)	(0.065)
Fut.VAT-incr. known, 1 Lag(s)	0.002	0.070	0.099*
	(0.045)	(0.051)	(0.059)
Fut.VAT-incr. known, 2 Lag(s)	0.058	0.139**	0.177***
	(0.060)	(0.063)	(0.066)
Fut.VAT-incr. known, 3 Lag(s)	0.004	0.075	0.117*
	(0.054)	(0.057)	(0.063)
Fut.VAT-incr. known, 4 Lag(s)	0.132	0.229**	0.248**
	(0.108)	(0.113)	(0.122)
Fut.VAT-incr. known, 5 Lag(s)	0.185	0.078	0.873
	(0.744)	(0.762)	(1.094)
Periods since last price change, $z(i_n, j, t,)$	0.014	0.028	0.026
	(0.019)	(0.026)	(0.026)
$z(i_n, j, t,)^2$	0.001*	0.001**	0.001**
	(0.001)	(0.001)	(0.001)
Dummy 1st quarter	0.285**	0.264**	0.260**
	(0.111)	(0.112)	(0.116)
Dummy 2nd quarter	0.156	0.189*	0.208**
	(0.099)	(0.098)	(0.104)
Dummy 3rd quarter	0.086	0.114	0.087
	(0.110)	(0.111)	(0.123)
Sales	18.924***	24.956***	23.915***
	(0.344)	(0.401)	(0.474)
Sales end	1.196	1.854*	1.834*
	(0.900)	(1.047)	(1.068)
Dummy 2000Q2	2.042***	1.887***	1.413***
	(0.236)	(0.244)	(0.296)
Acc.sec.infl., $\pi(i_n, j, t)$		0.010	0.009
		(0.046)	(0.049)
Price relative to mean price, $\rho(i_n, j, t \quad 1)$		0.125***	0.126***
		(0.009)	(0.009)
$\rho(i_n, j, t \quad 1)^2$		0.001***	0.001***
		(0.000)	(0.000)
GDP growth, yoy			0.018
			(0.068)
Lag 1 quarters			0.085
			(0.082)

Lag 2 quarters			0.052
			(0.087)
Lag 3 quarters			0.074
			(0.088)
Lag 4 quarters			0.002
			(0.059)
RER index, gr. qoq			0.010
			(0.017)
Lag 1 quarters			0.033*
			(0.020)
Lag 2 quarters			0.033
			(0.021)
Lag 3 quarters			0.024
			(0.021)
Lag 4 quarters			0.015
			(0.023)
3m LIBOR, 1st diff.			0.294*
			(0.164)
Lag 1 quarters			0.108
			(0.131)
Lag 2 quarters			0.297**
			(0.144)
Lag 3 quarters			0.009
			(0.171)
Lag 4 quarters			0.131
			(0.128)
Pseudo R^2	0.035	0.118	0.120
Observations	71,300	71,300	71,300

Standard errors in parentheses
* $p < 0.1$, ** $p < 0.05$, *** $p < 0.01$

An increase in the VAT has a positive effect on the probability of a positive price change, while this effect is only significant at the time of the increase itself or for as many as two lags before. After a VAT increase, the coefficient becomes insignificant or even negative. Unsurprisingly, the probability of a negative price change decreases as the VAT increases.

State-dependent factors (i.e., $\pi(i_n, j, t)$ and $\rho(i_n, j, t-1)$) are indicated to be of distinct importance in the pricing decision, as well as compared to time-dependent factors, in keeping with the literature (e.g., Klenow and Kryvtsov (2008)). However, accumulated inflation, $\pi(i_n, j, t)$, is only significant in the estimation of positive price changes, whereas the relative deviation from the mean price always affects the extensive pricing decision. The influence seems to be even stronger with regard to negative price changes, in which the inclusion of the variable notably leads to a remarkable increase in the goodness of the fit.

With exception of the interest rate, which has also a positive impact on the probability of a negative price change, macroeconomic factors only play roles in the estimation of positive price changes. Whereas the effect of the business cycle is rather unclear, we can observe a positive impact of the real exchange rate index and a change in the interest rate. Both results are interesting, because an appreciation of the home currency and an increase in the interest rate are intended to lead to a decrease in the price level. Recall that our data set is based on non-tradable services, which are not generally directly influenced by movements in the exchange rate. However, an appreciation of the home currency results in a decrease in the prices of imported goods, indicating that households' available incomes increase. This effect likely leads to a greater demand for non-tradable services as they are represented in our data set.[87] This increasing demand might be the reason for the positive impact of the real exchange rate index.

4.4.3 Pricing at the intensive margin

This section analyzes the pricing decisions of firms at the intensive margin. In this context, the intensive margin refers to the unconditional impact of our explanatory variables on the sizes of price changes. Thus, we perform OLS estimations, treating the size of price changes, $\hat{p}(i_n, j, t)$, as the dependent variable including data points with no price changes because these represent also relevant pricing decisions. Note that all the relative changes are expressed in percentages, allowing for a direct interpretation of the coefficients. Table 4.5 presents the results of

[87] In more technical terms: The income effect of an exchange rate fluctuation appears to dominate the substitution effect.

the three specifications. To make an example for proper interpretation, assume a one percent increase in the VAT. The coefficient in the first specification thus imply that prices rise on average by 0.992% according to our data sample, i.e., that those firms which really adjust prices must do that by a stronger degree than the coefficient suggests.

Regarding the time-dependent variables, we observe that the number of periods since the last price change has a significant, but small, impact on the size of a current price change. We also observe that the size of price changes (not only the probability) is larger in the first quarter of a year than in others. The observation that seasonality also plays a role at the intensive margin might to some degree be connected to wage contracts typically being renewed at the beginning of a calendar year in Switzerland.[88]

State-dependent factors also play more important roles at the intensive margin; however, the price development within a sector is of limited importance. If at all, only a small share of the general price evolution seems to be considered in the pricing decision. A better indicator might be represented by the deviation from the mean price, $\rho(i_n, j, t-1)$. The further from the mean that a price is, the stronger its correction is. However, with a coefficient of approximately -0.09, the impact is rather small in size, indicating that factors other than standing within the market (with regard to the price) play important roles.[89]

Contrary to the conditional logit model, we cannot discern a clear impact of the real exchange rate index when totaling the effects of all lags. An immediate positive effect is equalized after four lags. A possible interpretation might be that an immediate wealth effect becomes operative after a change in the exchange rate, which allows for an increase in prices. However, this effects fades and becomes dominated by a substitution effect after a few periods.

[88]cp. Fehr and Goette (2005).

[89]Note that we notably observe a positive coefficient on the squared variable, i.e., $\rho(i_n, j, t-1)^2$. However, this small effect, stating that the total impact is principally non-linear, never dominates the linear coefficient.

Furthermore, we observe evidence of pro-cyclical behavior in the size of price changes but with some lag. Finally, the interest rate has a (although small) negative impact on the average size of price changes. A F-test considering the sum of all coefficients as zero can be rejected.[90]

Table 4.5: Estimation results: Size of relative price change.

	Specification 1	Specification 2	Specification 3
Rel. change VAT	0.992***	0.999***	0.982***
	(0.048)	(0.047)	(0.049)
Rel.chan. VAT, 1 Lag(s)	0.039***	0.032***	0.010
	(0.012)	(0.012)	(0.017)
Rel.chan. VAT, 2 Lag(s)	0.033***	0.024***	0.017
	(0.007)	(0.008)	(0.013)
Fut.VAT-incr. known, 1 Lag(s)	0.082**	0.092***	0.080**
	(0.032)	(0.031)	(0.032)
Fut.VAT-incr. known, 2 Lag(s)	0.041***	0.055***	0.084***
	(0.015)	(0.015)	(0.017)
Fut.VAT-incr. known, 3 Lag(s)	0.000	0.012	0.066***
	(0.017)	(0.017)	(0.019)
Fut.VAT-incr. known, 4 Lag(s)	0.011	0.003	0.014
	(0.027)	(0.028)	(0.029)
Fut.VAT-incr. known, 5 Lag(s)	0.047	0.273	0.352
	(0.249)	(0.238)	(0.428)
Periods since last price change, $z(i_n, j, t,)$	0.046***	0.023***	0.016***
	(0.004)	(0.005)	(0.005)
$z(i_n, j, t,)^2$	0.000***	0.001***	0.001***
	(0.000)	(0.000)	(0.000)
Dummy 1st quarter	0.377***	0.396***	0.407***
	(0.035)	(0.034)	(0.039)
Dummy 2nd quarter	0.149***	0.128***	0.182***
	(0.033)	(0.032)	(0.039)
Dummy 3rd quarter	0.027	0.014	0.059*
	(0.026)	(0.026)	(0.033)
Sales	18.816***	18.367***	18.328***
	(2.219)	(2.206)	(2.243)
Sales end	16.258***	15.375***	15.401***
	(5.710)	(5.560)	(5.546)
Dummy 2000Q2	0.246	0.466	0.591*
	(0.331)	(0.324)	(0.329)

[90] The respective p-value is 0.036.

Acc.sec.infl., $\pi(i_n, j, t)$		0.006	0.029*
		(0.015)	(0.016)
Price relative to mean price, $\rho(i_n, j, t \quad 1)$		0.093***	0.093***
		(0.005)	(0.005)
$\rho(i_n, j, t \quad 1)^2$		0.001***	0.001***
		(0.000)	(0.000)
GDP growth, yoy			0.021
			(0.018)
Lag 1 quarters			0.019
			(0.026)
Lag 2 quarters			0.006
			(0.030)
Lag 3 quarters			0.004
			(0.027)
Lag 4 quarters			0.103***
			(0.016)
RER index, gr. qoq			0.033***
			(0.007)
Lag 1 quarters			0.025***
			(0.009)
Lag 2 quarters			0.012*
			(0.007)
Lag 3 quarters			0.025***
			(0.006)
Lag 4 quarters			0.031***
			(0.007)
3m LIBOR, 1st diff.			0.075*
			(0.044)
Lag 1 quarters			0.039
			(0.043)
Lag 2 quarters			0.027
			(0.046)
Lag 3 quarters			0.113**
			(0.048)
Lag 4 quarters			0.045
			(0.034)
Constant	0.138***	0.190***	0.362***
	(0.030)	(0.055)	(0.071)
Adjusted R^2	0.064	0.098	0.100
Observations	219,209	219,209	219,209
Sum VAT-coefficients$^{\phi}$	1.150	0.944	0.904
p-value$^{\phi\phi}$	0.586	0.834	0.826

Standard errors in parentheses
* $p < 0.1$, ** $p < 0.05$, *** $p < 0.01$
$^{\phi}$Sum-up of all VAT-related coefficients, i.e. of the first eight coefficients in each column.
$^{\phi\phi}$Null hypothesis: Sum of all VAT-related coefficients equals one.

4.4.4 The VAT

The introduction of the VAT in the year 1995 and the subsequent increases in 1999, 2001 and 2012 represent exogenous cost shocks to firms. Thus, all these increases at large are an ideal policy experiment to study the (size of) price changes by firms. The results in table 4.5 indicate that the total effect, i.e., the elasticity of the relative price change with regard to the relative change in the VAT, determined by totaling all the relevant coefficients, is not statistically different from one (or even greater than one) in any of its specifications.[91] This finding is at a first glance consistent with the hypothesis that firms increase their prices *pari passu* with the relative change in the VAT, i.e., the tax increase is directly reflected in the prices.

If every sector along the value chain of a product passes the VAT change proportionally into prices, it is optimal for a single firm to raise its price proportionally as well if it wants to keep its markup unchanged. To understand this relationship, let us write the price of a product as the sum of its marginal costs plus the markup. Marginal costs can be expressed as the sum of two components: the costs of input goods or services, denoted c_1, and the cost of the own added value, e.g., wages, interest rates, etc., denoted c_2. Thus, the price can be written as

$$p(i_n, j, t) := \left(\frac{c_1(i_n, j, t)}{1 + \tau_t} + c_2(i_n, j, t) \right) \mu(i_n, j, t)(1 + \tau_t), \tag{4.5}$$

where $\mu(i_n, j, t)$ denotes the markup factor. Assume that the markup factor is independent of τ_t. We guess that the input sectors raise their prices proportionally to the VAT increase, hence, c_1 is proportional to $1 + \tau_t$. Consequently, the optimal price $p(i_n, j, t)$ is proportional to $1 + \tau_t$ as well, confirming the initial guess.

[91] cp. the last two lines in table 4.5.

However, because our results indicate that average prices rise proportionally with the VAT increase, we can conclude that firms changing their prices, increase them more than one-to-one with the tax increase. As we control for firm-specific state variables, we can conclude that firms (that change their prices) seem to regard a VAT increase as an opportunity to increase their markup.

4.4.5 Endogeneity issues

In the estimations above, we found that macroeconomic factors have a clear causal effect. However, it is possible that shocks influencing macroeconomic variables, such as real GDP growth, also have an impact on the price setting considerations of firms, i.e., they are occasionally simultaneously determined.[92] This impact would cause an endogeneity problem, because the error terms in the estimations above are not uncorrelated with the regressors. As a result, our estimated coefficients might be inconsistent.

To address this possible bias, we re-estimate our chosen specifications using an instrumental variable (IV) approach. Recall that our price data series rely on non-tradable services. However, the Swiss economy in general is a typical example of a small open economy. Thus, it is clear that the macroeconomic or policy parameters of the most important trading partners (the European Union and the US) have impacts on macroeconomic conditions in Switzerland. A good example would be the short-term interest rates set by the respective central bank. They have direct impacts on the exchange rate and are therefore also correlated with the Swiss business cycle. Moreover, the short-term interest rate for the Swiss franc is also heavily influenced by the interest rates of Switzerland's most important trading partners. However, there is no reason to believe that non-trading firms consider

[92]Note that we do not consider the VAT to be a potentially endogenous variable, because the VAT is not used as an instrument to conduct macroeconomic policy in Switzerland. The setting of the VAT is the result of a political process, and the time of introduction/change is random. See Strittmatter and Sunde (2013) for a similar discussion of health insurance.

foreign central banking policy in their pricing decisions, making the short-term interest rates of the trading partners a valid instrument.

In the re-estimation, each macroeconomic variable is added separately to the standard regression and then is instrumented using the short-term interest rates (and their lags) of the European Union and the US.[93] This procedure also allows us also to determine whether our results are robust to the individual inclusion of the macroeconomic variables. For the non-linear conditional logit model, our estimation relies on the instrumental variable approach proposed by Terza et al. (2008). Note that standard errors in these estimations are bootstrapped to ensure that they remain consistent and comparable.[94] The estimation procedure for the linear standard TSLS estimation follows the procedure of Schaffer (2005) to obtain unbiased, clustered standard errors.

Tables 4.7 - 4.8 in appendix 4.A report the results of the IV regressions. As can be observed, the IV regressions generally tend to report stronger effects relative to the standard estimations with regard to the impact of macroeconomic factors (in both the conditional logit and the standard OLS model). This difference also holds for the impact of the interest rate on the relative price change, which is even more strongly negative in the IV regression. Moreover, the impact of the real exchange rate index is clearly positive in the IV regression. At a minimum, this finding provides us with an indication that regarding the impact of the real exchange rate index, in concretizing our results from the standard regressions in table 4.5, the income effect is likely to dominate in general, i.e., including over a longer time horizon.

---

[93] Data on the particular short-term interest rates are provided by the ECB and the FED, respectively.

[94] The bootstrapping procedure consists of 1,000 replications.

4.4.6 Additional robustness checks

In this section, we test whether our results are robust to data preconditions. First, we estimate our regressions by restricting the time frame considered to the period after 1995. With this restriction we exclude the introduction of the VAT, which can be considered an exceptional incident in the sense that the increase in the VAT was extraordinary high at this point in time (compared to other increases in the VAT), which might lead to overestimation of the effects of the VAT. Moreover, as we observed in the descriptive statistics section, the number of price changes was very high in 1995. The respective results can be found in appendix 4.B.1. Surprisingly, the effects of the VAT increase somewhat when considering the restricted time frame, whereas the impacts of the other variables remain approximately constant.

Second, we modify our data in the sense that we assume the first data point in each price series to be a price change, i.e., $k_1(i_n, j) \equiv t_1 \; \forall \, i, j$. This procedure expands the number of available data points, making the estimation more precise; however, Klenow and Kryvtsov (2008) argue that the results may become biased. Nevertheless, our results do not generally reflect a notable difference between the usage of two data types in the estimations. See appendix 4.B.2 for details.

Third, we perform our estimations separately for the four product groups (i.e., cinema tickets, hairdresser services, drinks at restaurants, and food at restaurants). The results in appendix 4.B.3 suggest that the impact of a change in the VAT is stronger in the restaurant and hairdresser sectors but is less pronounced for cinemas. Moreover, the impact of the real exchange rate appears indeterminate in the cinema sector, whereas the hairdresser sector is the most affected. However, these results are not surprising, because the cinema sector tends to change prices less frequently than the other sectors.

Overall, the robustness checks confirm our findings from the previous estimations. Time-dependent variables, with exception of the seasonality impact, play a less important role relative to state-dependent factors. This especially holds for the relative standing in the market, measured as the relative deviation from the mean price. Finally, the estimations provide evidence that changes in the VAT are taken as a chance by firms to increase the markup. The following section shows that changes in the VAT can also have an impact on the distributions of prices.

4.5 Price dispersion

A unique feature of our data set is that it allows us to estimate price dispersion (variance and higher moments) for each of the 73 product types at each point in time, further allowing us to analyze the factors that might influence the distribution of prices from a more macroeconomic perspective. For this purpose, we rely on the data on the relative deviation from the mean product price of each observed price, i.e., $\rho(i_n, j, t)$.

In particular, we denote

$$VAR(\rho(i,t)) := \frac{1}{A(i,t)} \sum_{n,j} \rho(i_n, j, t)^2 \tag{4.6}$$

as the variance,

$$SKE(\rho(i,t)) := \frac{1}{A(i,t)} \sum_{n,j} \rho(i_n, j, t)^3 \tag{4.7}$$

as the skewness, and

$$KUR(\rho(i,t)) := \frac{1}{A(i,t)} \sum_{n,j} \rho(i_n, j, t)^4 \tag{4.8}$$

as the kurtosis of the relative price of product i in period t.

Based on this calculation, we perform in a first specification (denoted as specification 1) a regression of the variance, the skewness and the kurtosis on their own first two lags, and on the change in the VAT. Furthermore, we again include dummies for the second quarter of 2000 and for the number of the quarter in each year. Additionally, we introduce a dummy for all periods after 2000Q2, because we might have a structural break after this point in time. In a second specification, we also add the year-on-year real GDP growth rate (denoted as specification 2). The estimation results are presented in table 4.6.

The results show that a rise in the VAT decreases the variance of prices. This may stem therefrom that firms charging relatively low prices vis-à-vis their competitors at the time of the VAT increase, raise their prices more strongly. Hence, they tend to regard this increase as an opportunity to close the gap relative to producers, which already charge high prices. This finding would also, to some extent, explain the puzzling finding from section 4.4.4, in which we found evidence that increases in the VAT are perceived as an opportunity for relatively high price increases. No significant impact can be observed regarding the business cycle, because the coefficients are jointly not different from zero.[95]

[95]The p-value of the respective F-test is 0.134. Note that the inclusion of other macroeconomic factors would not show any significant results either (i.e., even not for single coefficients).

Table 4.6: Estimation results for price dispersion.

Dep. variable, (specification)	$VAR(\rho(i,t))$, (1)	$VAR(\rho(i,t))$, (2)	$SKE(\rho(i,t))$, (1)	$SKE(\rho(i,t))$, (2)	$KUR(\rho(i,t))$, (1)	$KUR(\rho(i,t))$, (2)
Lag 1 period	0.653***	0.653***	0.801***	0.801***	0.668***	0.668***
	(0.148)	(0.148)	(0.0808)	(0.080)	(0.125)	(0.125)
Lag 2 period	0.212*	0.211*	0.097	0.096	0.179**	0.179**
	(0.120)	(0.120)	(0.066)	(0.066)	(0.085)	(0.085)
Rel. change VAT	−4.170**	−6.501***	−0.004	−0.006	−0.007	−0.022
	(1.738)	(2.067)	(0.004)	(0.005)	(0.031)	(0.039)
Dummy 1. quarter	5.824	6.876	−0.005	−0.004	−0.039	−0.029
	(9.190)	(9.139)	(0.015)	(0.015)	(0.092)	(0.094)
Dummy 2. quarter	−2.849	−2.807	0.001	0.001	0.049	0.052
	(10.485)	(10.714)	(0.011)	(0.011)	(0.065)	(0.065)
Dummy 3. quarter	−9.259	−8.873	0.018	0.018	0.170*	0.175*
	(8.093)	(8.249)	(0.014)	(0.014)	(0.097)	(0.098)
Dummy 2000Q2	274.377**	269.980**	0.428**	0.412**	2.518	2.447
	(133.988)	(134.362)	(0.167)	(0.170)	(1.580)	(1.593)
Post 2000Q2	13.412*	12.140	0.014	0.013	0.002	0.015
	(7.621)	(7.312)	(0.017)	(0.017)	(0.130)	(0.126)
GDP growth, yoy		−1.934		0.001		−0.010
		(3.560)		(0.007)		(0.040)
Lag 1 quarter		4.339		−0.004		−0.003
		(3.740)		(0.008)		(0.045)
Lag 2 quarters		1.023		0.011		0.050
		(3.439)		(0.010)		(0.058)
Lag 3 quarters		−7.629*		−0.012		−0.095
		(4.073)		(0.010)		(0.069)
Lag 4 quarters		5.839**		0.005		0.034
		(2.440)		(0.005)		(0.034)
Adjusted R^2	0.689	0.689	0.791	0.791	0.677	0.677

Robust standard errors in parentheses, * $p < 0.10$, ** $p < 0.05$, *** $p < 0.01$

4.6 Conclusion

Using a data set of the price series underlying the Swiss CPI, we analyzed the factors that influence the price setting behavior of firms and the price dispersion within a small open economy. Contrary to most previous research, our data set not only allowed us to investigate the factors that influence the frequency (i.e., the extensive margin) but also the (average) size of price changes (i.e., the intensive margin). Moreover, the development of individual prices can be observed over a relatively long period of time. We found that the time span between price changes is not particularly important in determining the sizes of price changes, supporting the finding reported in previous papers that time-dependent variables are of little importance. This finding does not apply to seasonality, because in agreement with numerous previous studies, we found that the frequency and size of price changes are highly seasonal, because firms generally tend to adjust prices at the beginning of the calendar year.

A unique strength of our dataset is that we can look at relevant state-dependent variables, and indeed they play an important role. Accumulated inflation between price changes has a clear impact; however, we observe an underproportional influence. More important is the relative standing in the market, measured as the relative deviation from the mean price of a specific product in the sample. Even more, this variable, which is constructed from the data, significantly improves the goodness of the fit of our estimations, although the absolut impact is rather small in size.

Furthermore, our results indicate that the influence of macroeconomic determinants on price setting behavior is rather small in size and in explanatory power. Nevertheless, we found some positive impacts of real GDP growth and the real exchange rate index at the extensive margin. The latter can be explained by our data set only consisting of the prices of non-tradable services. As imports become less expensive in response to a stronger home currency, the demand for this type of services can increase due to a dominating income effect. At a minimum, our IV regressions also support this hypothesis at the intensive margin. This result is of particular interest for models considering the impact of exchange rate movements on the general price level as there seem to be more effects at work than the simple pass-through. Moreover, we also found that a positive change in the short-term interest rate has a negative impact on both the probability and the size of a price change.

We placed an especial emphasis on the role of the VAT as an important policy parameter. Our results indicate that increases in the VAT raise the average price level proportionally implying that firms, that indeed adjust prices, do this over-proportionally. An increase in the VAT, which can be regarded as an external policy shock, may be interpreted as an opportunity for firms to increase their margins. This insight can notably help improving forecasts of price developments when it comes to changes in the VAT.

Finally, the data set also allowed us to estimate the price dispersion for each product category. By performing a regression of several moments on their lags, changes in the VAT, and the business cycle, we found some indication that an increase in the VAT reduces the variance of prices within an economy. It might be a nearby explanation that firms charging a relative low price take the VAT increase as a chance to narrow the gap to their competitors, however, a theoretical substantiation of the role of the VAT that elucidates our findings is left for future research.

Appendix

4.A IV regressions

The following tables present the results for the IV estimations. Model 1 includes real GDP growth, model 2 the relative change of the real exchange rate index, and model 3 the short-term interest rate (i.e., the first difference of the Swiss LIBOR). For each model, the three month LIBOR of the Euro area and of the US are used as instruments.

Table 4.7: Estimation results for IV regressions: Size of relative price changes.

Rel. price change	model1	model1IV	model2	model2IV	model3	model3IV
Rel. change VAT	0.988***	1.002***	0.985***	0.982***	1.002***	1.027***
	(0.047)	(0.048)	(0.048)	(0.054)	(0.047)	(0.048)
Rel.chan. VAT, 1 Lag(s)	0.031**	−0.028	0.002	−0.104***	0.017	0.003
	(0.013)	(0.021)	(0.013)	(0.022)	(0.012)	(0.015)
Rel.chan. VAT, 2 Lag(s)	0.029***	0.028	0.015	−0.083***	−0.000	−0.050***
	(0.010)	(0.019)	(0.010)	(0.026)	(0.010)	(0.014)
Fut.VAT-incr. known, 1 Lag(s)	0.097***	0.105***	0.083***	−0.037	0.095***	0.099***
	(0.032)	(0.034)	(0.030)	(0.033)	(0.031)	(0.031)
Fut.VAT-incr. known, 2 Lag(s)	0.058***	0.009	0.055***	0.039	0.065***	0.091***
	(0.016)	(0.021)	(0.016)	(0.032)	(0.015)	(0.015)
Fut.VAT-incr. known, 3 Lag(s)	0.040**	0.050**	0.012	−0.115***	0.029*	0.035**
	(0.018)	(0.021)	(0.018)	(0.030)	(0.017)	(0.018)
Fut.VAT-incr. known, 4 Lag(s)	0.039	0.093***	−0.014	−0.046	0.036	0.050*
	(0.028)	(0.030)	(0.029)	(0.031)	(0.027)	(0.029)
Fut.VAT-incr. known, 5 Lag(s)	0.214	0.988***	−0.114	−0.306	0.300	0.095
	(0.261)	(0.367)	(0.236)	(0.259)	(0.321)	(0.526)
Acc.sec.infl., $\pi(i_n, j, t)$	0.018	0.002	0.015	−0.040*	0.014	−0.014
	(0.015)	(0.017)	(0.015)	(0.022)	(0.015)	(0.016)
Periods since last price change, $z(i_n, j, t,)$	0.020***	0.030***	0.020***	0.048***	0.021***	0.037***
	(0.005)	(0.006)	(0.005)	(0.009)	(0.005)	(0.006)
$z(i_n, j, t,)^2$	−0.001***	−0.001***	−0.001***	−0.001***	−0.001***	−0.001***
	(0.000)	(0.000)	(0.000)	(0.000)	(0.000)	(0.000)
Dummy 1st quarter	0.413***	0.426***	0.404***	0.241***	0.364***	0.276***
	(0.036)	(0.036)	(0.037)	(0.078)	(0.033)	(0.036)
Dummy 2nd quarter	0.125***	0.165***	0.167***	0.220***	0.094***	0.060
	(0.034)	(0.039)	(0.034)	(0.042)	(0.034)	(0.041)
Dummy 3rd quarter	0.022	0.064**	0.038	−0.008	0.017	0.059
	(0.026)	(0.028)	(0.028)	(0.062)	(0.029)	(0.040)

Price relative to mean price, $\rho(i_n, j, t-1)$	−0.093***	−0.092***	−0.093***	−0.090***	−0.093***	−0.092***
	(0.005)	(0.005)	(0.005)	(0.005)	(0.005)	(0.005)
$\rho(i_n, j, t-1)^2$	0.001***	0.001***	0.001***	0.001***	0.001***	0.001***
	(0.000)	(0.000)	(0.000)	(0.000)	(0.000)	(0.000)
GDP growth, yoy	0.004	−0.014				
	(0.014)	(0.035)				
Lag 1 quarters	−0.021	−0.217***				
	(0.024)	(0.062)				
Lag 2 quarters	0.041	0.205***				
	(0.027)	(0.068)				
Lag 3 quarters	−0.023	0.024				
	(0.022)	(0.068)				
Lag 4 quarters	0.067***	0.024				
	(0.012)	(0.032)				
Sales	−18.316***	−18.353***	−18.369***	−18.405***	−18.374***	−18.462***
	(2.221)	(2.250)	(2.221)	(2.205)	(2.223)	(2.240)
Sales end	15.433***	15.532***	15.349***	15.444***	15.411***	15.443***
	(5.551)	(5.574)	(5.560)	(5.499)	(5.572)	(5.585)
Dummy 2000Q2	0.531	0.637*	0.432	0.770**	0.515	0.822**
	(0.327)	(0.327)	(0.319)	(0.320)	(0.325)	(0.344)
RER index, gr. qoq			0.024***	0.014		
			(0.006)	(0.029)		
Lag 1 quarters			0.027***	0.185***		
			(0.007)	(0.030)		
Lag 2 quarters			−0.002	0.009		
			(0.005)	(0.027)		
Lag 3 quarters			−0.014**	0.072***		
			(0.006)	(0.019)		
Lag 4 quarters			−0.016**	0.011		
			(0.006)	(0.023)		

3m LIBOR, 1st diff.					−0.073**	−0.392***
					(0.031)	(0.061)
Lag 1 quarters					−0.069**	−0.350***
					(0.032)	(0.078)
Lag 2 quarters					0.065**	0.098*
					(0.032)	(0.057)
Lag 3 quarters					0.108***	0.083
					(0.036)	(0.074)
Lag 4 quarters					0.127***	0.230***
					(0.025)	(0.044)
Adjusted R^2	0.099	0.050	0.098	0.039	0.098	0.050
Observations	219,209	219,012	219,209	219,012	219,209	219,012

Standard errors in parentheses
* $p < 0.1$, ** $p < 0.05$, *** $p < 0.01$

Table 4.8: Cond. logit probability model: IV regressions.

Panel A: Positive price changes	model1	model1IV	model2	model2IV	model3	model3IV
Rel. change VAT	0.709***	0.603***	0.662***	0.679***	0.735***	0.650***
	(0.051)	(0.062)	(0.051)	(0.053)	(0.052)	(0.052)
Rel.chan. VAT, 1 Lag(s)	−0.010	−0.100	−0.077	−0.192***	−0.030	0.092*
	(0.055)	(0.067)	(0.052)	(0.069)	(0.052)	(0.051)
Rel.chan. VAT, 2 Lag(s)	0.004	0.113	−0.069	−0.209***	−0.082	−0.228***
	(0.062)	(0.083)	(0.060)	(0.069)	(0.059)	(0.065)
Fut.VAT-incr. known, 1 Lag(s)	0.272***	0.428***	0.220***	0.021	0.269***	0.268***
	(0.054)	(0.067)	(0.053)	(0.068)	(0.053)	(0.069)
Fut.VAT-incr. known, 2 Lag(s)	0.184***	0.060	0.156**	0.226***	0.231***	0.116
	(0.059)	(0.065)	(0.061)	(0.080)	(0.059)	(0.073)

Fut.VAT-incr. known, 3 Lag(s)	0.029	0.120*	−0.062	−0.145	0.021	0.020
	(0.081)	(0.070)	(0.088)	(0.095)	(0.085)	(0.084)
Fut.VAT-incr. known, 4 Lag(s)	0.098*	0.199***	−0.075	0.074	0.113*	0.295***
	(0.058)	(0.071)	(0.072)	(0.068)	(0.058)	(0.074)
Fut.VAT-incr. known, 5 Lag(s)	1.750**	5.964***	0.431	1.163*	2.111**	1.831
	(0.692)	(1.386)	(0.615)	(0.706)	(0.848)	(1.491)
Periods since last price change, $z(i_n, j, t,)$	0.080***	0.092***	0.087***	0.115***	0.081***	0.130***
	(0.014)	(0.016)	(0.014)	(0.019)	(0.014)	(0.018)
$z(i_n, j, t,)^2$	−0.002***	−0.002***	−0.002***	−0.002***	−0.002***	−0.002***
	(0.000)	(0.000)	(0.000)	(0.000)	(0.000)	(0.000)
Dummy 1st quarter	1.371***	1.616***	1.357***	1.078***	1.234***	1.344***
	(0.097)	(0.118)	(0.101)	(0.117)	(0.090)	(0.133)
Dummy 2nd quarter	0.584***	0.870***	0.672***	0.729***	0.490***	0.131
	(0.104)	(0.134)	(0.104)	(0.114)	(0.107)	(0.122)
Dummy 3rd quarter	0.139	0.557***	0.209**	0.117	0.141	0.113
	(0.087)	(0.110)	(0.089)	(0.109)	(0.087)	(0.112)
Sales	−13.709***	−14.105***	−13.829***	−14.442***	−13.826***	−14.466***
	(0.451)	(0.984)	(0.520)	(0.904)	(0.471)	(0.861)
Sales end	2.941***	3.124***	2.703***	3.133***	2.864***	3.274***
	(0.497)	(0.913)	(0.478)	(0.566)	(0.499)	(0.563)
Dummy 2000Q2	1.205***	1.241***	1.123***	2.213***	1.066***	2.162***
	(0.182)	(0.302)	(0.163)	(0.217)	(0.169)	(0.303)
Acc.sec.infl., $\pi(i_n, j, t)$	0.140***	0.139***	0.103***	0.081	0.135***	0.031
	(0.035)	(0.034)	(0.036)	(0.051)	(0.035)	(0.037)
Price relative to mean price, $\rho(i_n, j, t-1)$	−0.072***	−0.072***	−0.072***	−0.069***	−0.072***	−0.070***
	(0.005)	(0.004)	(0.005)	(0.004)	(0.005)	(0.004)
$\rho(i_n, j, t-1)^2$	0.000**	0.000***	0.000**	0.000**	0.000**	0.000**
	(0.000)	(0.000)	(0.000)	(0.000)	(0.000)	(0.000)
GDP growth, yoy	−0.006	−0.772***				
	(0.033)	(0.247)				

Lag 1 quarters	−0.055	−0.604***				
	(0.052)	(0.067)				
Lag 2 quarters	0.134**	0.890***				
	(0.056)	(0.133)				
Lag 3 quarters	−0.037	−0.417***				
	(0.050)	(0.154)				
Lag 4 quarters	0.140***	0.517***				
	(0.032)	(0.112)				
RER index, gr. qoq			0.075***	0.223***		
			(0.014)	(0.036)		
Lag 1 quarters			0.098***	0.358***		
			(0.016)	(0.051)		
Lag 2 quarters			0.027*	−0.033		
			(0.014)	(0.038)		
Lag 3 quarters			−0.049***	0.104***		
			(0.014)	(0.038)		
Lag 4 quarters			−0.017	0.053		
			(0.014)	(0.041)		
3m LIBOR, 1st diff.					−0.211***	0.271***
					(0.060)	(0.045)
Lag 1 quarters					−0.221***	−0.781***
					(0.055)	(0.117)
Lag 2 quarters					0.389***	−0.139
					(0.081)	(0.192)
Lag 3 quarters					0.362***	0.743***
					(0.094)	(0.233)
Lag 4 quarters					0.358***	0.838***
					(0.066)	(0.114)
Pseudo R^2	0.196	0.211	0.195	0.209	0.196	0.202
Observations	180,032	180,032	180,032	180,032	180,032	180,032

Panel B: Negative price changes	model1	model1IV	model2	model2IV	model3	model3IV
Rel. change VAT	−0.079	−0.132**	−0.099**	−0.096*	−0.104**	−0.066
	(0.055)	(0.065)	(0.048)	(0.058)	(0.049)	(0.053)
Rel.chan. VAT, 1 Lag(s)	−0.278***	−0.309***	−0.273***	−0.297***	−0.248***	−0.264***
	(0.071)	(0.082)	(0.073)	(0.110)	(0.071)	(0.098)
Rel.chan. VAT, 2 Lag(s)	−0.132**	−0.074	−0.153***	−0.163**	−0.141**	−0.160**
	(0.060)	(0.081)	(0.058)	(0.074)	(0.059)	(0.066)
Fut.VAT-incr. known, 1 Lag(s)	−0.067	−0.004	−0.079	−0.111	−0.084	−0.079
	(0.050)	(0.071)	(0.057)	(0.078)	(0.054)	(0.058)
Fut.VAT-incr. known, 2 Lag(s)	−0.156**	−0.189**	−0.147**	−0.144	−0.135**	−0.083
	(0.062)	(0.076)	(0.065)	(0.091)	(0.064)	(0.075)
Fut.VAT-incr. known, 3 Lag(s)	−0.074	−0.072	−0.092	−0.106	−0.090	−0.083
	(0.059)	(0.067)	(0.058)	(0.087)	(0.060)	(0.061)
Fut.VAT-incr. known, 4 Lag(s)	−0.228**	−0.214	−0.234**	−0.223	−0.225*	−0.233
	(0.113)	(0.274)	(0.113)	(0.225)	(0.115)	(0.211)
Fut.VAT-incr. known, 5 Lag(s)	0.317	1.606	0.077	0.074	−0.714	−1.470
	(0.801)	(1.669)	(0.756)	(0.808)	(1.055)	(1.303)
Periods since last price change, $z(i_n, j, t,)$	0.021	0.030	0.032	0.037	0.018	0.019
	(0.026)	(0.028)	(0.026)	(0.031)	(0.026)	(0.029)
$z(i_n, j, t,)^2$	0.001**	0.001**	0.001**	0.001**	0.002**	0.002**
	(0.001)	(0.001)	(0.001)	(0.001)	(0.001)	(0.001)
Dummy 1st quarter	0.271**	0.356***	0.252**	0.222	0.258**	0.131
	(0.109)	(0.122)	(0.117)	(0.151)	(0.106)	(0.129)
Dummy 2nd quarter	0.204**	0.306**	0.187*	0.206*	0.201**	0.177
	(0.100)	(0.133)	(0.099)	(0.108)	(0.102)	(0.109)
Dummy 3rd quarter	0.128	0.226	0.124	0.099	0.068	0.021
	(0.108)	(0.168)	(0.120)	(0.141)	(0.117)	(0.140)
Sales	24.964***	22.255***	24.984***	22.191***	23.995***	22.074***
	(0.402)	(2.767)	(0.399)	(2.954)	(0.455)	(2.904)

Sales end	1.859*	1.855	1.868*	1.896	1.821*	1.846
	(1.052)	(4.591)	(1.047)	(4.887)	(1.065)	(4.862)
Dummy 2000Q2	1.784***	1.600***	1.948***	2.024***	1.568***	1.473***
	(0.286)	(0.397)	(0.247)	(0.298)	(0.258)	(0.388)
Acc.sec.infl., $\pi(i_n, j, t)$	0.005	−0.010	−0.020	−0.027	0.010	0.011
	(0.048)	(0.057)	(0.048)	(0.062)	(0.047)	(0.057)
Price relative to mean price, $\rho(i_n, j, t-1)$	0.125***	0.125***	0.125***	0.126***	0.125***	0.125***
	(0.009)	(0.009)	(0.009)	(0.010)	(0.009)	(0.009)
$\rho(i_n, j, t-1)^2$	−0.001***	−0.001***	−0.001***	−0.001***	−0.001***	−0.001***
	(0.000)	(0.000)	(0.000)	(0.000)	(0.000)	(0.000)
GDP growth, yoy	0.047	−0.198				
	(0.056)	(0.286)				
Lag 1 quarters	−0.060	−0.163**				
	(0.082)	(0.078)				
Lag 2 quarters	0.059	0.330*				
	(0.086)	(0.190)				
Lag 3 quarters	−0.009	−0.215				
	(0.092)	(0.190)				
Lag 4 quarters	−0.007	0.113				
	(0.055)	(0.127)				
RER index, gr. qoq			−0.003	0.019		
			(0.016)	(0.052)		
Lag 1 quarters			0.016	0.047		
			(0.018)	(0.062)		
Lag 2 quarters			0.014	−0.003		
			(0.018)	(0.049)		
Lag 3 quarters			0.006	0.030		
			(0.016)	(0.051)		
Lag 4 quarters			0.008	0.013		
			(0.017)	(0.047)		

3m LIBOR, 1st diff.					0.163	−0.061
					(0.108)	(0.049)
Lag 1 quarters					−0.001	−0.230
					(0.099)	(0.144)
Lag 2 quarters					0.147	0.257
					(0.097)	(0.207)
Lag 3 quarters					−0.125	−0.308
					(0.124)	(0.220)
Lag 4 quarters					0.051	0.137
					(0.087)	(0.142)
Pseudo R^2	0.118	0.118	0.118	0.118	0.119	0.119
Observations	71,300	71,300	71,300	71,300	71,300	71,300

Standard errors in parentheses

* $p < 0.1$, ** $p < 0.05$, *** $p < 0.01$

4.B Additional robustness checks

4.B.1 Reduced time frame

The following tables show the estimation results using a shorted time frame (i.e., 1996Q1-2012Q4).

Table 4.9: Estimation results with restricted time frame: Size of relative price change.

	Specification 1	Specification 2	Specification 3
Rel. change VAT	1.696***	1.877***	1.700***
	(0.213)	(0.214)	(0.211)
Rel.chan. VAT, 1 Lag(s)	0.145**	0.026	0.000
	(0.069)	(0.071)	(0.088)
Rel.chan. VAT, 2 Lag(s)	0.302**	0.472***	0.478***
	(0.121)	(0.117)	(0.128)
Fut.VAT-incr. known, 1 Lag(s)	0.135*	0.033	0.154*
	(0.072)	(0.073)	(0.083)
Fut.VAT-incr. known, 2 Lag(s)	0.013	0.155*	0.316***
	(0.083)	(0.084)	(0.095)
Fut.VAT-incr. known, 3 Lag(s)	0.312***	0.171**	0.125
	(0.069)	(0.073)	(0.103)
Fut.VAT-incr. known, 4 Lag(s)	0.755***	0.697***	0.539
	(0.255)	(0.255)	(0.413)
Fut.VAT-incr. known, 5 Lag(s)	0.077	0.234	0.563
	(0.251)	(0.238)	(0.425)
Periods since last price change, $z(i_n, j, t,)$	0.047***	0.033***	0.027***
	(0.004)	(0.005)	(0.006)
$z(i_n, j, t,)^2$	0.000***	0.001***	0.001***
	(0.000)	(0.000)	(0.000)
Dummy 1st quarter	0.346***	0.355***	0.359***
	(0.037)	(0.036)	(0.044)
Dummy 2nd quarter	0.198***	0.159***	0.185***
	(0.038)	(0.037)	(0.046)
Dummy 3rd quarter	0.009	0.020	0.007
	(0.028)	(0.027)	(0.036)
Sales	18.795***	18.264***	18.228***
	(2.223)	(2.213)	(2.236)
Sales end	16.304***	15.384***	15.384***
	(5.741)	(5.581)	(5.567)
Dummy 2000Q2	0.229	0.472	0.668**
	(0.330)	(0.321)	(0.327)

Acc.sec.infl., $\pi(i_n, j, t)$		0.044***	0.023
		(0.014)	(0.014)
Price relative to mean price, $\rho(i_n, j, t \quad 1)$		0.099***	0.099***
		(0.005)	(0.005)
$\rho(i_n, j, t \quad 1)^2$		0.000***	0.000***
		(0.000)	(0.000)
GDP growth, yoy			0.001
			(0.019)
Lag 1 quarters			0.018
			(0.027)
Lag 2 quarters			0.053*
			(0.030)
Lag 3 quarters			0.008
			(0.034)
Lag 4 quarters			0.091***
			(0.020)
RER index, gr. qoq			0.028***
			(0.008)
Lag 1 quarters			0.030***
			(0.008)
Lag 2 quarters			0.019**
			(0.008)
Lag 3 quarters			0.026***
			(0.006)
Lag 4 quarters			0.028***
			(0.008)
3m LIBOR, 1st diff.			0.080*
			(0.041)
Lag 1 quarters			0.024
			(0.042)
Lag 2 quarters			0.013
			(0.049)
Lag 3 quarters			0.100*
			(0.055)
Lag 4 quarters			0.059
			(0.046)
Constant	0.142***	0.190***	0.304***
	(0.034)	(0.057)	(0.073)
Adjusted R^2	0.028	0.065	0.067
Observations	198,989	198,989	198,989

Standard errors in parentheses
* $p < 0.1$, ** $p < 0.05$, *** $p < 0.01$

Table 4.10: Cond. logit probability model with restricted time frame.

Panel A: Positive price changes	Specification 1	Specification 2	Specification 3
Rel. change VAT	1.868***	2.214***	1.636***
	(0.141)	(0.156)	(0.193)
Rel.chan. VAT, 1 Lag(s)	0.925***	0.821**	1.154***
	(0.310)	(0.325)	(0.415)
Rel.chan. VAT, 2 Lag(s)	0.923***	1.097***	0.987***
	(0.245)	(0.256)	(0.312)
Fut.VAT-incr. known, 1 Lag(s)	0.617	0.366	0.924**
	(0.405)	(0.413)	(0.417)
Fut.VAT-incr. known, 2 Lag(s)	0.260	0.518**	0.875***
	(0.246)	(0.257)	(0.271)
Fut.VAT-incr. known, 3 Lag(s)	1.078***	0.859**	0.011
	(0.341)	(0.353)	(0.391)
Fut.VAT-incr. known, 4 Lag(s)	1.672***	1.625***	1.366
	(0.515)	(0.504)	(0.963)
Fut.VAT-incr. known, 5 Lag(s)	0.109	0.244	0.590
	(0.605)	(0.600)	(1.078)
Periods since last price change, $z(i_n, j, t,)$	0.114***	0.079***	0.089***
	(0.011)	(0.014)	(0.014)
$z(i_n, j, t,)^2$	0.001**	0.001***	0.001***
	(0.000)	(0.000)	(0.000)
Dummy 1st quarter	1.130***	1.156***	1.067***
	(0.103)	(0.104)	(0.118)
Dummy 2nd quarter	0.665***	0.630***	0.566***
	(0.101)	(0.100)	(0.121)
Dummy 3rd quarter	0.031	0.064	0.029
	(0.090)	(0.091)	(0.105)
Sales	13.830***	13.919***	13.818***
	(0.481)	(0.521)	(0.483)
Sales end	3.272***	2.817***	2.823***
	(0.572)	(0.544)	(0.502)
Dummy 2000Q2	0.869***	1.073***	1.377***
	(0.149)	(0.158)	(0.214)
Acc.sec.infl., $\pi(i_n, j, t)$		0.070**	0.062*
		(0.035)	(0.034)
Price relative to mean price, $\rho(i_n, j, t \quad 1)$		0.078***	0.081***
		(0.005)	(0.005)
$\rho(i_n, j, t \quad 1)^2$		0.000**	0.000**
		(0.000)	(0.000)
GDP growth, yoy			0.006
			(0.044)

Lag 1 quarters			0.040
			(0.070)
Lag 2 quarters			0.085
			(0.066)
Lag 3 quarters			0.200***
			(0.077)
Lag 4 quarters			0.275***
			(0.052)
RER index, gr. qoq			0.095***
			(0.016)
Lag 1 quarters			0.103***
			(0.020)
Lag 2 quarters			0.016
			(0.018)
Lag 3 quarters			0.024
			(0.017)
Lag 4 quarters			0.031*
			(0.018)
3m LIBOR, 1st diff.			0.214**
			(0.108)
Lag 1 quarters			0.067
			(0.115)
Lag 2 quarters			0.388***
			(0.106)
Lag 3 quarters			0.170
			(0.129)
Lag 4 quarters			0.108
			(0.134)
Pseudo R^2	0.127	0.153	0.169
Observations	158,057	158,057	158,057
Panel B: Negative price changes	Specification 1	Specification 2	Specification 3
Rel. change VAT	0.636***	0.445**	0.299
	(0.207)	(0.217)	(0.253)
Rel.chan. VAT, 1 Lag(s)	1.389***	1.382***	1.521***
	(0.396)	(0.390)	(0.450)
Rel.chan. VAT, 2 Lag(s)	0.366	0.277	0.134
	(0.273)	(0.265)	(0.302)
Fut.VAT-incr. known, 1 Lag(s)	1.198***	1.337***	1.452***
	(0.340)	(0.327)	(0.393)
Fut.VAT-incr. known, 2 Lag(s)	0.339	0.208	0.168
	(0.363)	(0.361)	(0.412)
Fut.VAT-incr. known, 3 Lag(s)	0.192	0.302	0.535
	(0.397)	(0.389)	(0.439)

Fut.VAT-incr. known, 4 Lag(s)	0.912	0.690	1.456
	(0.657)	(0.706)	(1.294)
Fut.VAT-incr. known, 5 Lag(s)	0.393	0.174	1.074
	(0.749)	(0.765)	(1.170)
Periods since last price change, $z(i_n, j, t,)$	0.015	0.031	0.036
	(0.019)	(0.027)	(0.027)
$z(i_n, j, t,)^2$	0.001**	0.002**	0.002**
	(0.001)	(0.001)	(0.001)
Dummy 1st quarter	0.187	0.131	0.138
	(0.120)	(0.120)	(0.135)
Dummy 2nd quarter	0.168	0.172*	0.213*
	(0.106)	(0.101)	(0.112)
Dummy 3rd quarter	0.043	0.034	0.040
	(0.121)	(0.119)	(0.135)
Sales	18.449***	24.144***	23.560***
	(0.348)	(0.411)	(0.465)
Sales end	1.190	1.753*	1.743
	(0.891)	(1.056)	(1.077)
Dummy 2000Q2	1.986***	1.838***	1.442***
	(0.237)	(0.247)	(0.305)
Acc.sec.infl., $\pi(i_n, j, t)$		0.029	0.043
		(0.049)	(0.053)
Price relative to mean price, $\rho(i_n, j, t \quad 1)$		0.126***	0.127***
		(0.009)	(0.009)
$\rho(i_n, j, t \quad 1)^2$		0.001***	0.001***
		(0.000)	(0.000)
GDP growth, yoy			0.002
			(0.073)
Lag 1 quarters			0.037
			(0.088)
Lag 2 quarters			0.024
			(0.090)
Lag 3 quarters			0.114
			(0.100)
Lag 4 quarters			0.021
			(0.065)
RER index, gr. qoq			0.009
			(0.019)
Lag 1 quarters			0.043**
			(0.020)
Lag 2 quarters			0.045**
			(0.020)
Lag 3 quarters			0.034
			(0.022)

Lag 4 quarters			0.018
			(0.023)
3m LIBOR, 1st diff.			0.220
			(0.161)
Lag 1 quarters			0.183
			(0.132)
Lag 2 quarters			0.320**
			(0.162)
Lag 3 quarters			0.079
			(0.183)
Lag 4 quarters			0.119
			(0.160)
Pseudo R^2	0.040	0.125	0.128
Observations	65,010	65,010	65,010

Standard errors in parentheses
* $p < 0.1$, ** $p < 0.05$, *** $p < 0.01$

4.B.2 Results with censored data

The following tables present the estimation results for a modified dataset, where we have assumed $k_1(i_n, j) \equiv t_1 \; \forall \, i, j$, i.e., the first datapoint of each price series is considered as a price change.

Table 4.11: Estimation results with censored data: Size of relative price change.

	Specification 1	Specification 2	Specification 3
Rel. change VAT	1.075***	1.065***	1.057***
	(0.041)	(0.040)	(0.043)
Rel.chan. VAT, 1 Lag(s)	0.072***	0.048***	0.027
	(0.019)	(0.017)	(0.021)
Rel.chan. VAT, 2 Lag(s)	0.042***	0.020**	0.020
	(0.008)	(0.009)	(0.013)
Fut.VAT-incr. known, 1 Lag(s)	0.101***	0.098***	0.097***
	(0.019)	(0.019)	(0.021)
Fut.VAT-incr. known, 2 Lag(s)	0.068***	0.065***	0.097***
	(0.015)	(0.015)	(0.018)
Fut.VAT-incr. known, 3 Lag(s)	0.050***	0.045***	0.095***
	(0.015)	(0.015)	(0.017)
Fut.VAT-incr. known, 4 Lag(s)	0.088***	0.069***	0.069***
	(0.018)	(0.017)	(0.019)
Fut.VAT-incr. known, 5 Lag(s)	0.169	0.442*	0.379
	(0.235)	(0.228)	(0.425)
Periods since last price change, $z(i_n, j, t,)$	0.047***	0.010**	0.001
	(0.004)	(0.004)	(0.005)
$z(i_n, j, t,)^2$	0.001***	0.001***	0.001***
	(0.000)	(0.000)	(0.000)
Dummy 1st quarter	0.351***	0.383***	0.407***
	(0.036)	(0.034)	(0.038)
Dummy 2nd quarter	0.135***	0.113***	0.199***
	(0.032)	(0.031)	(0.037)
Dummy 3rd quarter	0.001	0.010	0.061**
	(0.026)	(0.025)	(0.030)
Sales	19.252***	18.862***	18.833***
	(2.353)	(2.380)	(2.435)
Sales end	16.681***	15.623***	15.662***
	(5.844)	(5.640)	(5.638)
Dummy 2000Q2	0.739*	0.977**	1.069**
	(0.430)	(0.419)	(0.429)
Acc.sec.infl., $\pi(i_n, j, t)$		0.038***	0.063***
		(0.011)	(0.011)

Price relative to mean price, $\rho(i_n, j, t \ \ 1)$		0.099***	0.099***
		(0.005)	(0.005)
$\rho(i_n, j, t \ \ 1)^2$		0.000***	0.000***
		(0.000)	(0.000)
GDP growth, yoy			0.034*
			(0.017)
Lag 1 quarters			0.025
			(0.028)
Lag 2 quarters			0.000
			(0.030)
Lag 3 quarters			0.000
			(0.026)
Lag 4 quarters			0.115***
			(0.014)
RER index, gr. qoq			0.034***
			(0.007)
Lag 1 quarters			0.022***
			(0.008)
Lag 2 quarters			0.014*
			(0.007)
Lag 3 quarters			0.030***
			(0.006)
Lag 4 quarters			0.038***
			(0.006)
3m LIBOR, 1st diff.			0.091**
			(0.040)
Lag 1 quarters			0.040
			(0.042)
Lag 2 quarters			0.037
			(0.043)
Lag 3 quarters			0.144***
			(0.046)
Lag 4 quarters			0.072**
			(0.030)
Constant	0.131***	0.153**	0.400***
	(0.029)	(0.062)	(0.072)
Adjusted R^2	0.092	0.128	0.130
Observations	314,803	314,803	314,803

Standard errors in parentheses
* $p < 0.1$, ** $p < 0.05$, *** $p < 0.01$

Table 4.12: Cond. logit probability model with censored data.

Panel A: Positive price changes	Specification 1	Specification 2	Specification 3
Rel. change VAT	0.633***	0.630***	0.537***
	(0.025)	(0.027)	(0.037)
Rel.chan. VAT, 1 Lag(s)	0.123***	0.073*	0.003
	(0.044)	(0.039)	(0.043)
Rel.chan. VAT, 2 Lag(s)	0.068	0.029	0.042
	(0.044)	(0.044)	(0.049)
Fut.VAT-incr. known, 1 Lag(s)	0.265***	0.245***	0.250***
	(0.033)	(0.033)	(0.044)
Fut.VAT-incr. known, 2 Lag(s)	0.167***	0.147***	0.204***
	(0.040)	(0.040)	(0.044)
Fut.VAT-incr. known, 3 Lag(s)	0.095**	0.074*	0.161***
	(0.040)	(0.039)	(0.041)
Fut.VAT-incr. known, 4 Lag(s)	0.143***	0.103***	0.118***
	(0.028)	(0.028)	(0.035)
Fut.VAT-incr. known, 5 Lag(s)	0.042	0.254	0.210
	(0.591)	(0.590)	(1.011)
Periods since last price change, $z(i_n, j, t,)$	0.120***	0.072***	0.062***
	(0.009)	(0.011)	(0.010)
$z(i_n, j, t,)^2$	0.001***	0.002***	0.002***
	(0.000)	(0.000)	(0.000)
Dummy 1st quarter	1.228***	1.290***	1.251***
	(0.087)	(0.087)	(0.098)
Dummy 2nd quarter	0.551***	0.537***	0.566***
	(0.093)	(0.092)	(0.104)
Dummy 3rd quarter	0.103	0.094	0.239***
	(0.083)	(0.083)	(0.089)
Sales	14.721***	13.797***	13.645***
	(0.487)	(0.508)	(0.415)
Sales end	3.381***	2.807***	2.949***
	(0.605)	(0.531)	(0.500)
Dummy 2000Q2	0.854***	1.045***	1.163***
	(0.147)	(0.149)	(0.192)
Acc.sec.infl., $\pi(i_n, j, t)$		0.128***	0.178***
		(0.025)	(0.026)
Price relative to mean price, $\rho(i_n, j, t \quad 1)$		0.071***	0.072***
		(0.004)	(0.004)
$\rho(i_n, j, t \quad 1)^2$		0.000**	0.000**
		(0.000)	(0.000)
GDP growth, yoy			0.048
			(0.039)

Lag 1 quarters			0.030
			(0.066)
Lag 2 quarters			0.030
			(0.064)
Lag 3 quarters			0.175***
			(0.060)
Lag 4 quarters			0.291***
			(0.036)
RER index, gr. qoq			0.098***
			(0.014)
Lag 1 quarters			0.099***
			(0.017)
Lag 2 quarters			0.013
			(0.018)
Lag 3 quarters			0.043***
			(0.016)
Lag 4 quarters			0.039**
			(0.016)
3m LIBOR, 1st diff.			0.105
			(0.092)
Lag 1 quarters			0.171*
			(0.099)
Lag 2 quarters			0.367***
			(0.088)
Lag 3 quarters			0.006
			(0.111)
Lag 4 quarters			0.048
			(0.087)
Pseudo R^2	0.189	0.216	0.238
Observations	270,384	270,384	270,384

Panel B: Negative price changes	Specification 1	Specification 2	Specification 3
Rel. change VAT	0.010	0.055	0.116**
	(0.032)	(0.033)	(0.052)
Rel.chan. VAT, 1 Lag(s)	0.184***	0.209***	0.275***
	(0.065)	(0.067)	(0.070)
Rel.chan. VAT, 2 Lag(s)	0.080	0.104**	0.147***
	(0.050)	(0.052)	(0.057)
Fut.VAT-incr. known, 1 Lag(s)	0.026	0.071**	0.105**
	(0.033)	(0.036)	(0.046)
Fut.VAT-incr. known, 2 Lag(s)	0.116*	0.182***	0.236***
	(0.060)	(0.060)	(0.064)
Fut.VAT-incr. known, 3 Lag(s)	0.013	0.091**	0.135***
	(0.034)	(0.035)	(0.045)

Fut.VAT-incr. known, 4 Lag(s)	0.107**	0.179***	0.198***
	(0.045)	(0.048)	(0.052)
Fut.VAT-incr. known, 5 Lag(s)	0.201	0.248	0.536
	(0.709)	(0.734)	(1.060)
Periods since last price change, $z(i_n, j, t,)$	0.002	0.026	0.021
	(0.017)	(0.021)	(0.020)
$z(i_n, j, t,)^2$	0.001*	0.001**	0.001**
	(0.001)	(0.001)	(0.001)
Dummy 1st quarter	0.320***	0.339***	0.311***
	(0.099)	(0.102)	(0.110)
Dummy 2nd quarter	0.170*	0.242**	0.234**
	(0.093)	(0.095)	(0.101)
Dummy 3rd quarter	0.113	0.171	0.109
	(0.104)	(0.108)	(0.117)
Sales	20.507***	25.528***	24.654***
	(0.343)	(0.356)	(0.404)
Sales end	1.392	2.212**	2.176**
	(0.881)	(1.029)	(1.052)
Dummy 2000Q2	2.043***	1.881***	1.286***
	(0.215)	(0.220)	(0.268)
Acc.sec.infl., $\pi(i_n, j, t)$		0.027	0.034
		(0.036)	(0.036)
Price relative to mean price, $\rho(i_n, j, t \quad 1)$		0.120***	0.122***
		(0.008)	(0.008)
$\rho(i_n, j, t \quad 1)^2$		0.001***	0.001***
		(0.000)	(0.000)
GDP growth, yoy			0.017
			(0.065)
Lag 1 quarters			0.108
			(0.079)
Lag 2 quarters			0.081
			(0.082)
Lag 3 quarters			0.120
			(0.082)
Lag 4 quarters			0.011
			(0.053)
RER index, gr. qoq			0.017
			(0.017)
Lag 1 quarters			0.040**
			(0.020)
Lag 2 quarters			0.037*
			(0.021)
Lag 3 quarters			0.034*
			(0.019)

Lag 4 quarters			0.016
			(0.021)
3m LIBOR, 1st diff.			0.328**
			(0.156)
Lag 1 quarters			0.138
			(0.125)
Lag 2 quarters			0.344**
			(0.134)
Lag 3 quarters			0.134
			(0.141)
Lag 4 quarters			0.221**
			(0.096)
Pseudo R^2	0.034	0.118	0.122
Observations	96,446	96,446	96,446

Standard errors in parentheses
* $p < 0.1$, ** $p < 0.05$, *** $p < 0.01$

4.B.3 Estimations for separated product groups

The tables in the subsequent sections show the regression results (at the intensive and the extensive margin) for the four product groups, Ω, separately. These product groups are hairdressers, cinemas food in restaurants, and drinks in restaurants. Note that the variable indicating sales might be excluded due to too few observations.

Hairdressers

Table 4.13: Regressions for relative price changes, hairdresser-sector.

	Specification 1	Specification 2	Specification 3
Rel. change VAT	0.909***	0.929***	0.879***
	(0.082)	(0.082)	(0.084)
Rel.chan. VAT, 1 Lag(s)	0.126***	0.143***	0.054*
	(0.038)	(0.030)	(0.032)
Rel.chan. VAT, 2 Lag(s)	0.020	0.017	0.007
	(0.013)	(0.017)	(0.023)
Fut.VAT-incr. known, 1 Lag(s)	0.009	0.012	0.024
	(0.012)	(0.016)	(0.029)

Fut.VAT-incr. known, 2 Lag(s)	0.007	0.035*	0.035
	(0.017)	(0.020)	(0.026)
Fut.VAT-incr. known, 3 Lag(s)	0.010	0.041	0.090***
	(0.024)	(0.026)	(0.031)
Fut.VAT-incr. known, 4 Lag(s)	0.013	0.029	0.047
	(0.074)	(0.075)	(0.075)
Fut.VAT-incr. known, 5 Lag(s)	0.906	1.290*	3.062***
	(0.741)	(0.748)	(0.973)
Periods since last price change, $z(i_n, j, t,)$	0.066***	0.013	0.042
	(0.010)	(0.027)	(0.028)
$z(i_n, j, t,)^2$	0.001***	0.001***	0.001***
	(0.000)	(0.000)	(0.000)
Dummy 1st quarter	0.747***	0.805***	0.836***
	(0.088)	(0.088)	(0.090)
Dummy 2nd quarter	0.021	0.063	0.014
	(0.044)	(0.051)	(0.059)
Dummy 3rd quarter	0.079	0.047	0.188**
	(0.049)	(0.048)	(0.077)
Sales	14.171***	13.649***	14.137***
	(0.076)	(0.102)	(0.146)
Sales end	10.287***	10.198***	10.539***
	(0.072)	(0.083)	(0.194)
Dummy 2000Q2	0.222	0.588	0.528
	(0.437)	(0.450)	(0.480)
Acc.sec.infl., $\pi(i_n, j, t)$		0.181**	0.268***
		(0.083)	(0.087)
Price relative to mean price, $\rho(i_n, j, t \quad 1)$		0.045***	0.044***
		(0.006)	(0.006)
$\rho(i_n, j, t \quad 1)^2$		0.000***	0.000***
		(0.000)	(0.000)
GDP growth, yoy			0.002
			(0.030)
Lag 1 quarters			0.115**
			(0.051)
Lag 2 quarters			0.085
			(0.072)
Lag 3 quarters			0.088
			(0.065)
Lag 4 quarters			0.101***
			(0.038)
RER index, gr. qoq			0.046***
			(0.016)
Lag 1 quarters			0.048***
			(0.012)

Lag 2 quarters			0.007
			(0.014)
Lag 3 quarters			0.028*
			(0.014)
Lag 4 quarters			0.040***
			(0.014)
3m LIBOR, 1st diff.			0.009
			(0.089)
Lag 1 quarters			0.151
			(0.099)
Lag 2 quarters			0.245***
			(0.088)
Lag 3 quarters			0.229**
			(0.109)
Lag 4 quarters			0.093
			(0.076)
Constant	0.254***	0.171**	0.107
	(0.053)	(0.075)	(0.136)
Adjusted R^2	0.133	0.150	0.156
Observations	26,021	26,021	26,021

Standard errors in parentheses
* $p < 0.1$, ** $p < 0.05$, *** $p < 0.01$

Table 4.14: Cond. logit probability model, hairdresser-sector.

Panel A: Positive price changes	Specification 1	Specification 2	Specification 3
Rel. change VAT	0.520***	0.553***	0.397***
	(0.078)	(0.082)	(0.097)
Rel.chan. VAT, 1 Lag(s)	0.393***	0.364***	0.127*
	(0.075)	(0.058)	(0.071)
Rel.chan. VAT, 2 Lag(s)	0.188	0.176	0.066
	(0.147)	(0.143)	(0.138)
Fut.VAT-incr. known, 1 Lag(s)	0.524	0.356	0.256
	(0.598)	(0.343)	(0.470)
Fut.VAT-incr. known, 2 Lag(s)	0.190**	0.208**	0.230**
	(0.094)	(0.098)	(0.110)
Fut.VAT-incr. known, 3 Lag(s)	0.162	0.181	0.322**
	(0.143)	(0.141)	(0.152)
Fut.VAT-incr. known, 4 Lag(s)	0.150	0.153	0.217**
	(0.098)	(0.098)	(0.101)
Fut.VAT-incr. known, 5 Lag(s)	2.476*	3.042**	7.767***
	(1.504)	(1.515)	(2.506)
Periods since last price change, $z(i_n, j, t,)$	0.246***	0.154***	0.068
	(0.030)	(0.045)	(0.044)

$z(i_n, j, t,)^2$	0.004***	0.005***	0.005***
	(0.001)	(0.001)	(0.001)
Dummy 1st quarter	2.084***	2.186***	2.187***
	(0.199)	(0.196)	(0.205)
Dummy 2nd quarter	0.329	0.253	0.027
	(0.259)	(0.254)	(0.275)
Dummy 3rd quarter	0.065	0.049	0.304
	(0.269)	(0.262)	(0.278)
Sales	11.138***	9.900***	10.375***
	(1.007)	(1.023)	(1.004)
Sales end	11.569***	10.680***	11.011***
	(1.002)	(1.021)	(1.162)
Dummy 2000Q2	0.846***	1.202***	0.785*
	(0.321)	(0.325)	(0.453)
Acc.sec.infl., $\pi(i_n, j, t)$		0.246**	0.521***
		(0.115)	(0.104)
Price relative to mean price, $\rho(i_n, j, t \quad 1)$		0.038***	0.044***
		(0.008)	(0.009)
$\rho(i_n, j, t \quad 1)^2$		0.000**	0.000***
		(0.000)	(0.000)
GDP growth, yoy			0.052
			(0.109)
Lag 1 quarters			0.348**
			(0.173)
Lag 2 quarters			0.460***
			(0.154)
Lag 3 quarters			0.611***
			(0.144)
Lag 4 quarters			0.282***
			(0.096)
RER index, gr. qoq			0.120***
			(0.037)
Lag 1 quarters			0.188***
			(0.035)
Lag 2 quarters			0.096*
			(0.050)
Lag 3 quarters			0.071*
			(0.038)
Lag 4 quarters			0.078
			(0.061)
3m LIBOR, 1st diff.			0.146
			(0.240)
Lag 1 quarters			0.230
			(0.227)

Lag 2 quarters			0.953***
			(0.240)
Lag 3 quarters			0.897**
			(0.374)
Lag 4 quarters			0.420
			(0.267)
Pseudo R^2	0.301	0.312	0.361
Observations	21,389	21,389	21,389
Panel B: Negative price changes	Specification 1	Specification 2	Specification 3
Rel. change VAT	0.379**	0.382**	0.215
	(0.185)	(0.185)	(0.261)
Rel.chan. VAT, 1 Lag(s)	0.978*	1.263***	1.088
	(0.553)	(0.438)	(0.752)
Rel.chan. VAT, 2 Lag(s)	0.304	0.363**	0.223
	(0.187)	(0.156)	(0.195)
Fut.VAT-incr. known, 1 Lag(s)	1.073	0.879**	0.993
	(0.821)	(0.421)	(1.000)
Fut.VAT-incr. known, 2 Lag(s)	0.297	0.303	0.245
	(0.255)	(0.249)	(0.291)
Fut.VAT-incr. known, 3 Lag(s)	0.145	0.231*	0.279**
	(0.104)	(0.132)	(0.131)
Fut.VAT-incr. known, 4 Lag(s)	0.382	0.494*	0.534*
	(0.273)	(0.285)	(0.284)
Fut.VAT-incr. known, 5 Lag(s)	33.500***	33.247***	32.771***
	(1.111)	(1.349)	(3.800)
Periods since last price change, $z(i_n, j, t,)$	0.057	0.197	0.135
	(0.075)	(0.173)	(0.161)
$z(i_n, j, t,)^2$	0.003	0.002	0.002
	(0.003)	(0.003)	(0.003)
Dummy 1st quarter	0.897*	0.982*	0.825
	(0.501)	(0.516)	(0.714)
Dummy 2nd quarter	0.842***	0.814**	0.588
	(0.306)	(0.323)	(0.456)
Dummy 3rd quarter	0.038	0.139	0.082
	(0.334)	(0.346)	(0.528)
Dummy 2000Q2	1.153**	1.214**	1.256
	(0.557)	(0.551)	(0.826)
Acc.sec.infl., $\pi(i_n, j, t)$		0.670*	0.520*
		(0.378)	(0.292)
Price relative to mean price, $\rho(i_n, j, t \quad 1)$		0.094***	0.083**
		(0.034)	(0.033)
$\rho(i_n, j, t \quad 1)^2$		0.000	0.000
		(0.000)	(0.000)

GDP growth, yoy			0.010
			(0.157)
Lag 1 quarters			0.198
			(0.302)
Lag 2 quarters			0.520
			(0.421)
Lag 3 quarters			0.065
			(0.400)
Lag 4 quarters			0.095
			(0.174)
RER index, gr. qoq			0.071
			(0.082)
Lag 1 quarters			0.006
			(0.070)
Lag 2 quarters			0.139
			(0.158)
Lag 3 quarters			0.018
			(0.100)
Lag 4 quarters			0.067
			(0.093)
3m LIBOR, 1st diff.			0.093
			(0.618)
Lag 1 quarters			1.135*
			(0.609)
Lag 2 quarters			1.064**
			(0.444)
Lag 3 quarters			1.738***
			(0.673)
Lag 4 quarters			0.125
			(0.312)
Pseudo R^2	0.097	0.189	0.249
Observations	3,902	3,902	3,902

Standard errors in parentheses
* $p < 0.1$, ** $p < 0.05$, *** $p < 0.01$

Cinemas

Table 4.15: Regressions for relative price changes, cinema-sector.

	Specification 1	Specification 2	Specification 3
Rel. change VAT	0.766***	0.765***	0.764***
	(0.106)	(0.102)	(0.103)

Rel.chan. VAT, 1 Lag(s)	0.026*	0.008	0.042
	(0.013)	(0.016)	(0.051)
Rel.chan. VAT, 2 Lag(s)	0.062**	0.051*	0.073*
	(0.025)	(0.026)	(0.039)
Fut.VAT-incr. known, 1 Lag(s)	0.046	0.050	0.091**
	(0.033)	(0.035)	(0.044)
Fut.VAT-incr. known, 2 Lag(s)	0.027	0.036	0.019
	(0.039)	(0.041)	(0.040)
Fut.VAT-incr. known, 3 Lag(s)	0.000	0.012	0.032
	(0.055)	(0.058)	(0.060)
Fut.VAT-incr. known, 4 Lag(s)	0.189	0.207	0.208
	(0.244)	(0.240)	(0.241)
Fut.VAT-incr. known, 5 Lag(s)	1.226***	1.106***	0.769
	(0.288)	(0.258)	(1.594)
Periods since last price change, $z(i_n, j, t,)$	0.047***	0.033***	0.037***
	(0.006)	(0.009)	(0.011)
$z(i_n, j, t,)^2$	0.001***	0.001***	0.001***
	(0.000)	(0.000)	(0.000)
Dummy 1st quarter	0.234**	0.250**	0.285***
	(0.104)	(0.102)	(0.103)
Dummy 2nd quarter	0.052	0.050	0.030
	(0.092)	(0.091)	(0.088)
Dummy 3rd quarter	0.101*	0.103*	0.035
	(0.060)	(0.058)	(0.086)
Dummy 2000Q2	0.246	0.179	0.279
	(0.251)	(0.239)	(0.320)
Acc.sec.infl., $\pi(i_n, j, t)$		0.010	0.017
		(0.020)	(0.020)
Price relative to mean price, $\rho(i_n, j, t \quad 1)$		0.102***	0.101***
		(0.014)	(0.014)
$\rho(i_n, j, t \quad 1)^2$		0.000**	0.000**
		(0.000)	(0.000)
GDP growth, yoy			0.046
			(0.061)
Lag 1 quarters			0.164
			(0.111)
Lag 2 quarters			0.183*
			(0.102)
Lag 3 quarters			0.123
			(0.084)
Lag 4 quarters			0.036
			(0.053)
RER index, gr. qoq			0.009
			(0.018)

Lag 1 quarters			0.045**
			(0.020)
Lag 2 quarters			0.016
			(0.014)
Lag 3 quarters			0.038**
			(0.018)
Lag 4 quarters			0.014
			(0.016)
3m LIBOR, 1st diff.			0.138
			(0.106)
Lag 1 quarters			0.007
			(0.086)
Lag 2 quarters			0.101
			(0.125)
Lag 3 quarters			0.114
			(0.252)
Lag 4 quarters			0.021
			(0.107)
Constant	0.178**	0.080	0.073
	(0.067)	(0.082)	(0.138)
Adjusted R^2	0.049	0.087	0.090
Observations	9,465	9,465	9,465

Standard errors in parentheses
* $p < 0.1$, ** $p < 0.05$, *** $p < 0.01$

Table 4.16: Cond. logit probability model, cinema-sector.

Panel A: Positive price changes	Specification 1	Specification 2	Specification 3
Rel. change VAT	0.623***	0.671***	0.671***
	(0.061)	(0.069)	(0.119)
Rel.chan. VAT, 1 Lag(s)	0.823	0.685	0.827
	(0.614)	(0.558)	(0.505)
Rel.chan. VAT, 2 Lag(s)	0.240***	0.221**	0.192
	(0.082)	(0.089)	(0.124)
Fut.VAT-incr. known, 1 Lag(s)	0.143	0.144	0.178
	(0.156)	(0.148)	(0.175)
Fut.VAT-incr. known, 2 Lag(s)	0.051	0.071	0.059
	(0.226)	(0.191)	(0.199)
Fut.VAT-incr. known, 3 Lag(s)	0.126	0.023	0.158
	(0.320)	(0.229)	(0.153)
Fut.VAT-incr. known, 4 Lag(s)	0.183	0.227**	0.205*
	(0.120)	(0.111)	(0.106)
Fut.VAT-incr. known, 5 Lag(s)	4.620	4.623	4.169
	(2.915)	(2.952)	(4.740)

Periods since last price change, $z(i_n, j, t,)$	0.136***	0.137***	0.155***
	(0.029)	(0.032)	(0.038)
$z(i_n, j, t,)^2$	0.001	0.002**	0.003***
	(0.001)	(0.001)	(0.001)
Dummy 1st quarter	0.774***	0.816***	0.805***
	(0.214)	(0.218)	(0.298)
Dummy 2nd quarter	0.144	0.226	0.276
	(0.266)	(0.264)	(0.285)
Dummy 3rd quarter	0.413	0.442*	0.251
	(0.259)	(0.254)	(0.279)
Dummy 2000Q2	0.316	0.554	0.701
	(0.687)	(0.662)	(0.905)
Acc.sec.infl., $\pi(i_n, j, t)$		0.064	0.074
		(0.056)	(0.057)
Price relative to mean price, $\rho(i_n, j, t \quad 1)$		0.142***	0.141***
		(0.018)	(0.017)
$\rho(i_n, j, t \quad 1)^2$		0.000***	0.000***
		(0.000)	(0.000)
GDP growth, yoy			0.258
			(0.188)
Lag 1 quarters			0.511*
			(0.266)
Lag 2 quarters			0.224
			(0.249)
Lag 3 quarters			0.201
			(0.216)
Lag 4 quarters			0.056
			(0.137)
RER index, gr. qoq			0.156***
			(0.040)
Lag 1 quarters			0.035
			(0.049)
Lag 2 quarters			0.055
			(0.040)
Lag 3 quarters			0.115***
			(0.043)
Lag 4 quarters			0.004
			(0.045)
3m LIBOR, 1st diff.			0.392
			(0.365)
Lag 1 quarters			0.074
			(0.308)
Lag 2 quarters			0.472
			(0.322)

Lag 3 quarters			0.680
			(0.505)
Lag 4 quarters			0.135
			(0.400)
Pseudo R^2	0.180	0.231	0.262
Observations	8,207	8,207	8,207
Panel B: Negative price changes	Specification 1	Specification 2	Specification 3
Rel. change VAT	0.303**	0.264*	0.066
	(0.131)	(0.143)	(0.168)
Rel.chan. VAT, 1 Lag(s)	7.728	5.011*	7.405*
	(5.530)	(2.731)	(4.370)
Rel.chan. VAT, 2 Lag(s)	0.058	0.126	0.027
	(0.076)	(0.083)	(0.181)
Fut.VAT-incr. known, 1 Lag(s)	0.140	0.204	0.079
	(0.178)	(0.242)	(0.262)
Fut.VAT-incr. known, 2 Lag(s)	0.016	0.035	0.084
	(0.233)	(0.288)	(0.297)
Fut.VAT-incr. known, 3 Lag(s)	0.162	0.239	0.617**
	(0.212)	(0.206)	(0.253)
Fut.VAT-incr. known, 4 Lag(s)	0.206	0.163	0.053
	(0.163)	(0.140)	(0.226)
Fut.VAT-incr. known, 5 Lag(s)	3.512	3.534*	0.256
	(2.479)	(1.968)	(3.031)
Periods since last price change, $z(i_n, j, t,)$	0.044	0.083	0.043
	(0.043)	(0.076)	(0.067)
$z(i_n, j, t,)^2$	0.000	0.000	0.001
	(0.001)	(0.003)	(0.002)
Dummy 1st quarter	0.800	0.736	0.012
	(0.499)	(0.504)	(0.530)
Dummy 2nd quarter	0.683	0.728	0.748
	(0.575)	(0.604)	(0.528)
Dummy 3rd quarter	0.703	0.725	1.246***
	(0.498)	(0.481)	(0.477)
Dummy 2000Q2	1.391**	0.834	0.141
	(0.669)	(1.078)	(1.347)
Acc.sec.infl., $\pi(i_n, j, t)$		0.170	0.121
		(0.130)	(0.151)
Price relative to mean price, $\rho(i_n, j, t\quad 1)$		0.314***	0.305***
		(0.063)	(0.060)
$\rho(i_n, j, t\quad 1)^2$		0.002	0.002
		(0.002)	(0.002)
GDP growth, yoy			0.959***
			(0.326)

Lag 1 quarters			0.881***
			(0.325)
Lag 2 quarters			0.328
			(0.361)
Lag 3 quarters			0.144
			(0.383)
Lag 4 quarters			0.480**
			(0.205)
RER index, gr. qoq			0.500***
			(0.080)
Lag 1 quarters			0.121
			(0.135)
Lag 2 quarters			0.091
			(0.131)
Lag 3 quarters			0.300**
			(0.119)
Lag 4 quarters			0.405***
			(0.096)
3m LIBOR, 1st diff.			0.425
			(0.828)
Lag 1 quarters			0.105
			(0.532)
Lag 2 quarters			2.144***
			(0.517)
Lag 3 quarters			0.403
			(0.519)
Lag 4 quarters			0.240
			(0.429)
Pseudo R^2	0.052	0.245	0.385
Observations	3,160	3,160	3,160

Standard errors in parentheses
* $p < 0.1$, ** $p < 0.05$, *** $p < 0.01$

Food in restaurants

Table 4.17: Regressions for relative price changes, restaurant-food-sector.

	Specification 1	Specification 2	Specification 3
Rel. change VAT	0.951***	0.957***	0.946***
	(0.059)	(0.057)	(0.060)
Rel.chan. VAT, 1 Lag(s)	0.021	0.014	0.002
	(0.015)	(0.015)	(0.024)

Rel.chan. VAT, 2 Lag(s)	0.031***	0.020**	0.008
	(0.009)	(0.010)	(0.017)
Fut.VAT-incr. known, 1 Lag(s)	0.113**	0.129***	0.099**
	(0.051)	(0.048)	(0.048)
Fut.VAT-incr. known, 2 Lag(s)	0.040*	0.056**	0.095***
	(0.023)	(0.026)	(0.028)
Fut.VAT-incr. known, 3 Lag(s)	0.002	0.010	0.057
	(0.036)	(0.037)	(0.040)
Fut.VAT-incr. known, 4 Lag(s)	0.008	0.005	0.008
	(0.026)	(0.030)	(0.031)
Fut.VAT-incr. known, 5 Lag(s)	0.103	0.487	1.422**
	(0.409)	(0.404)	(0.633)
Periods since last price change, $z(i_n, j, t,)$	0.041***	0.023***	0.017**
	(0.006)	(0.007)	(0.008)
$z(i_n, j, t,)^2$	0.000***	0.001***	0.001***
	(0.000)	(0.000)	(0.000)
Dummy 1st quarter	0.206***	0.218***	0.204***
	(0.053)	(0.052)	(0.060)
Dummy 2nd quarter	0.172***	0.140***	0.188***
	(0.047)	(0.046)	(0.055)
Dummy 3rd quarter	0.001	0.018	0.009
	(0.034)	(0.033)	(0.045)
Sales	19.318***	18.823***	18.778***
	(3.469)	(3.482)	(3.511)
Sales end	18.855**	17.914**	17.959**
	(8.950)	(8.665)	(8.641)
Dummy 2000Q2	0.114	0.386	0.480
	(0.699)	(0.684)	(0.698)
Acc.sec.infl., $\pi(i_n, j, t)$		0.004	0.016
		(0.022)	(0.025)
Price relative to mean price, $\rho(i_n, j, t \quad 1)$		0.101***	0.100***
		(0.007)	(0.007)
$\rho(i_n, j, t \quad 1)^2$		0.000***	0.000***
		(0.000)	(0.000)
GDP growth, yoy			0.030
			(0.023)
Lag 1 quarters			0.012
			(0.037)
Lag 2 quarters			0.042
			(0.043)
Lag 3 quarters			0.001
			(0.039)
Lag 4 quarters			0.104***
			(0.022)

RER index, gr. qoq			0.026***
			(0.010)
Lag 1 quarters			0.026**
			(0.011)
Lag 2 quarters			0.006
			(0.009)
Lag 3 quarters			0.008
			(0.008)
Lag 4 quarters			0.030***
			(0.010)
3m LIBOR, 1st diff.			0.046
			(0.057)
Lag 1 quarters			0.003
			(0.063)
Lag 2 quarters			0.080
			(0.066)
Lag 3 quarters			0.181***
			(0.065)
Lag 4 quarters			0.034
			(0.054)
Constant	0.066	0.265***	0.391***
	(0.045)	(0.073)	(0.097)
Adjusted R^2	0.045	0.082	0.083
Observations	91,769	91,769	91,769

Standard errors in parentheses
* $p < 0.1$, ** $p < 0.05$, *** $p < 0.01$

Table 4.18: Cond. logit probability model, restaurant-food-sector.

Panel A: Positive price changes	Specification 1	Specification 2	Specification 3
Rel. change VAT	0.725***	0.751***	0.658***
	(0.059)	(0.066)	(0.065)
Rel.chan. VAT, 1 Lag(s)	0.020	0.045	0.112
	(0.067)	(0.064)	(0.072)
Rel.chan. VAT, 2 Lag(s)	0.001	0.027	0.084
	(0.081)	(0.081)	(0.089)
Fut.VAT-incr. known, 1 Lag(s)	0.229***	0.221***	0.203***
	(0.058)	(0.057)	(0.063)
Fut.VAT-incr. known, 2 Lag(s)	0.151**	0.141**	0.197***
	(0.071)	(0.071)	(0.070)
Fut.VAT-incr. known, 3 Lag(s)	0.023	0.031	0.057
	(0.114)	(0.107)	(0.092)
Fut.VAT-incr. known, 4 Lag(s)	0.073	0.111	0.040
	(0.127)	(0.131)	(0.103)

Fut.VAT-incr. known, 5 Lag(s)	0.308	0.086	0.005
	(0.681)	(0.682)	(1.205)
Periods since last price change, $z(i_n, j, t,)$	0.086***	0.061***	0.054***
	(0.014)	(0.017)	(0.018)
$z(i_n, j, t,)^2$	0.000	0.001**	0.001***
	(0.000)	(0.000)	(0.000)
Dummy 1st quarter	0.831***	0.856***	0.821***
	(0.125)	(0.125)	(0.147)
Dummy 2nd quarter	0.517***	0.502***	0.532***
	(0.124)	(0.124)	(0.148)
Dummy 3rd quarter	0.059	0.052	0.115
	(0.101)	(0.101)	(0.113)
Sales	12.516***	12.882***	12.632***
	(0.401)	(0.392)	(0.378)
Sales end	2.814***	2.372***	2.540***
	(0.643)	(0.584)	(0.555)
Dummy 2000Q2	0.835***	0.997***	1.035***
	(0.230)	(0.241)	(0.265)
Acc.sec.infl., $\pi(i_n, j, t)$		0.062	0.097*
		(0.049)	(0.052)
Price relative to mean price, $\rho(i_n, j, t \quad 1)$		0.068***	0.068***
		(0.007)	(0.007)
$\rho(i_n, j, t \quad 1)^2$		0.000***	0.000***
		(0.000)	(0.000)
GDP growth, yoy			0.003
			(0.049)
Lag 1 quarters			0.013
			(0.075)
Lag 2 quarters			0.038
			(0.079)
Lag 3 quarters			0.155**
			(0.078)
Lag 4 quarters			0.211***
			(0.046)
RER index, gr. qoq			0.057***
			(0.017)
Lag 1 quarters			0.094***
			(0.022)
Lag 2 quarters			0.014
			(0.019)
Lag 3 quarters			0.017
			(0.019)
Lag 4 quarters			0.029
			(0.021)

3m LIBOR, 1st diff.			0.004
			(0.114)
Lag 1 quarters			0.035
			(0.147)
Lag 2 quarters			0.319***
			(0.113)
Lag 3 quarters			0.042
			(0.148)
Lag 4 quarters			0.120
			(0.112)
Pseudo R^2	0.113	0.137	0.153
Observations	72,919	72,919	72,919

Panel B: Negative price changes	Specification 1	Specification 2	Specification 3
Rel. change VAT	0.028	0.032	0.076
	(0.056)	(0.059)	(0.070)
Rel.chan. VAT, 1 Lag(s)	0.129*	0.164**	0.213**
	(0.067)	(0.074)	(0.087)
Rel.chan. VAT, 2 Lag(s)	0.125*	0.167**	0.181**
	(0.071)	(0.069)	(0.075)
Fut.VAT-incr. known, 1 Lag(s)	0.032	0.042	0.041
	(0.053)	(0.053)	(0.067)
Fut.VAT-incr. known, 2 Lag(s)	0.030	0.118*	0.140**
	(0.066)	(0.070)	(0.069)
Fut.VAT-incr. known, 3 Lag(s)	0.014	0.054	0.082
	(0.062)	(0.067)	(0.072)
Fut.VAT-incr. known, 4 Lag(s)	0.184	0.233	0.204
	(0.168)	(0.148)	(0.146)
Fut.VAT-incr. known, 5 Lag(s)	0.508	0.807	0.985
	(0.896)	(0.941)	(1.469)
Periods since last price change, $z(i_n, j, t,)$	0.030	0.015	0.013
	(0.023)	(0.033)	(0.033)
$z(i_n, j, t,)^2$	0.002**	0.002***	0.002***
	(0.001)	(0.001)	(0.001)
Dummy 1st quarter	0.219*	0.190	0.183
	(0.122)	(0.124)	(0.127)
Dummy 2nd quarter	0.048	0.075	0.069
	(0.106)	(0.107)	(0.112)
Dummy 3rd quarter	0.130	0.150	0.104
	(0.101)	(0.102)	(0.122)
Sales	20.987***	24.303***	22.882***
	(0.403)	(0.525)	(0.571)
Sales end	0.747	1.350	1.304
	(1.099)	(1.285)	(1.281)

Dummy 2000Q2	2.265***	2.064***	1.575***
	(0.266)	(0.275)	(0.331)
Acc.sec.infl., $\pi(i_n, j, t)$		0.056	0.054
		(0.064)	(0.069)
Price relative to mean price, $\rho(i_n, j, t \quad 1)$		0.108***	0.108***
		(0.010)	(0.010)
$\rho(i_n, j, t \quad 1)^2$		0.000***	0.000***
		(0.000)	(0.000)
GDP growth, yoy			0.035
			(0.067)
Lag 1 quarters			0.091
			(0.092)
Lag 2 quarters			0.123
			(0.099)
Lag 3 quarters			0.124
			(0.095)
Lag 4 quarters			0.014
			(0.060)
RER index, gr. qoq			0.000
			(0.018)
Lag 1 quarters			0.036*
			(0.021)
Lag 2 quarters			0.004
			(0.023)
Lag 3 quarters			0.017
			(0.021)
Lag 4 quarters			0.009
			(0.025)
3m LIBOR, 1st diff.			0.281*
			(0.156)
Lag 1 quarters			0.065
			(0.153)
Lag 2 quarters			0.258*
			(0.152)
Lag 3 quarters			0.175
			(0.200)
Lag 4 quarters			0.191
			(0.135)
Pseudo R^2	0.037	0.111	0.113
Observations	34,298	34,298	34,298

Standard errors in parentheses

* $p < 0.1$, ** $p < 0.05$, *** $p < 0.01$

Drinks in restaurants

Table 4.19: Regressions for relative price changes, restaurant-drinks-sector.

	Specification 1	Specification 2	Specification 3
Rel. change VAT	1.070***	1.076***	1.058***
	(0.070)	(0.068)	(0.071)
Rel.chan. VAT, 1 Lag(s)	0.027**	0.008	0.007
	(0.012)	(0.012)	(0.020)
Rel.chan. VAT, 2 Lag(s)	0.033***	0.016	0.010
	(0.009)	(0.011)	(0.020)
Fut.VAT-incr. known, 1 Lag(s)	0.105**	0.109***	0.100**
	(0.042)	(0.040)	(0.044)
Fut.VAT-incr. known, 2 Lag(s)	0.060**	0.062**	0.101***
	(0.028)	(0.028)	(0.030)
Fut.VAT-incr. known, 3 Lag(s)	0.003	0.003	0.077***
	(0.017)	(0.018)	(0.021)
Fut.VAT-incr. known, 4 Lag(s)	0.028	0.045	0.019
	(0.029)	(0.033)	(0.035)
Fut.VAT-incr. known, 5 Lag(s)	0.065	0.286	0.061
	(0.322)	(0.306)	(0.528)
Periods since last price change, $z(i_n, j, t,)$	0.043***	0.021***	0.010
	(0.005)	(0.007)	(0.008)
$z(i_n, j, t,)^2$	0.000*	0.001***	0.001***
	(0.000)	(0.000)	(0.000)
Dummy 1st quarter	0.472***	0.492***	0.525***
	(0.043)	(0.042)	(0.047)
Dummy 2nd quarter	0.187***	0.177***	0.234***
	(0.044)	(0.042)	(0.048)
Dummy 3rd quarter	0.057	0.048	0.105**
	(0.038)	(0.037)	(0.042)
Sales	18.312***	17.910***	17.840***
	(3.616)	(3.458)	(3.520)
Sales end	13.994***	12.884***	12.824***
	(5.269)	(4.897)	(4.904)
Dummy 2000Q2	0.458	0.584*	0.791**
	(0.318)	(0.307)	(0.317)
Acc.sec.infl., $\pi(i_n, j, t)$		0.004	0.036
		(0.022)	(0.023)
Price relative to mean price, $\rho(i_n, j, t \quad 1)$		0.102***	0.103***
		(0.006)	(0.006)
$\rho(i_n, j, t \quad 1)^2$		0.000***	0.000***
		(0.000)	(0.000)

GDP growth, yoy			0.018
			(0.025)
Lag 1 quarters			0.003
			(0.035)
Lag 2 quarters			0.010
			(0.043)
Lag 3 quarters			0.026
			(0.036)
Lag 4 quarters			0.106***
			(0.021)
RER index, gr. qoq			0.043***
			(0.010)
Lag 1 quarters			0.025**
			(0.012)
Lag 2 quarters			0.023**
			(0.009)
Lag 3 quarters			0.050***
			(0.008)
Lag 4 quarters			0.036***
			(0.010)
3m LIBOR, 1st diff.			0.112*
			(0.064)
Lag 1 quarters			0.102*
			(0.056)
Lag 2 quarters			0.052
			(0.062)
Lag 3 quarters			0.144**
			(0.067)
Lag 4 quarters			0.032
			(0.044)
Constant	0.165***	0.164***	0.414***
	(0.041)	(0.053)	(0.081)
Adjusted R^2	0.083	0.121	0.126
Observations	91,954	91,954	91,954

Standard errors in parentheses
* $p < 0.1$, ** $p < 0.05$, *** $p < 0.01$

Table 4.20: Cond. logit probability model, restaurant-drinks-sector.

Panel A: Positive price changes	Specification 1	Specification 2	Specification 3
Rel. change VAT	0.797***	0.852***	0.675***
	(0.086)	(0.109)	(0.092)
Rel.chan. VAT, 1 Lag(s)	0.067	0.118	0.158*
	(0.095)	(0.093)	(0.094)

Rel.chan. VAT, 2 Lag(s)	0.040	0.084	0.200***
	(0.066)	(0.065)	(0.078)
Fut.VAT-incr. known, 1 Lag(s)	0.359***	0.352***	0.312***
	(0.069)	(0.067)	(0.077)
Fut.VAT-incr. known, 2 Lag(s)	0.247***	0.239***	0.325***
	(0.083)	(0.081)	(0.081)
Fut.VAT-incr. known, 3 Lag(s)	0.329	0.235	0.062
	(0.263)	(0.186)	(0.098)
Fut.VAT-incr. known, 4 Lag(s)	0.226	0.282	0.113
	(0.170)	(0.189)	(0.096)
Fut.VAT-incr. known, 5 Lag(s)	0.739	1.081	1.807
	(1.129)	(1.120)	(1.641)
Periods since last price change, $z(i_n, j, t,)$	0.138***	0.099***	0.094***
	(0.014)	(0.018)	(0.018)
$z(i_n, j, t,)^2$	0.001**	0.002***	0.003***
	(0.000)	(0.000)	(0.000)
Dummy 1st quarter	1.549***	1.608***	1.638***
	(0.125)	(0.122)	(0.137)
Dummy 2nd quarter	0.813***	0.779***	0.827***
	(0.134)	(0.130)	(0.150)
Dummy 3rd quarter	0.218*	0.201	0.390***
	(0.129)	(0.128)	(0.135)
Sales	13.163***	14.454***	14.023***
	(0.831)	(0.881)	(0.841)
Sales end	4.188***	3.598***	3.475***
	(0.913)	(0.666)	(0.703)
Dummy 2000Q2	1.018***	1.156***	1.715***
	(0.198)	(0.211)	(0.314)
Acc.sec.infl., $\pi(i_n, j, t)$		0.124**	0.157***
		(0.049)	(0.049)
Price relative to mean price, $\rho(i_n, j, t \quad 1)$		0.090***	0.094***
		(0.006)	(0.007)
$\rho(i_n, j, t \quad 1)^2$		0.000***	0.000***
		(0.000)	(0.000)
GDP growth, yoy			0.057
			(0.062)
Lag 1 quarters			0.046
			(0.096)
Lag 2 quarters			0.183*
			(0.099)
Lag 3 quarters			0.039
			(0.089)
Lag 4 quarters			0.303***
			(0.054)

RER index, gr. qoq			0.144***
			(0.021)
Lag 1 quarters			0.097***
			(0.027)
Lag 2 quarters			0.003
			(0.027)
Lag 3 quarters			0.080***
			(0.024)
Lag 4 quarters			0.013
			(0.026)
3m LIBOR, 1st diff.			0.202
			(0.174)
Lag 1 quarters			0.106
			(0.153)
Lag 2 quarters			0.359**
			(0.143)
Lag 3 quarters			0.066
			(0.187)
Lag 4 quarters			0.111
			(0.132)
Pseudo R^2	0.195	0.224	0.256
Observations	77,517	77,517	77,517

Panel B: Negative price changes	Specification 1	Specification 2	Specification 3
Rel. change VAT	0.074	0.150**	0.274***
	(0.073)	(0.068)	(0.099)
Rel.chan. VAT, 1 Lag(s)	0.338**	0.384**	0.352***
	(0.157)	(0.160)	(0.135)
Rel.chan. VAT, 2 Lag(s)	0.036	0.082	0.152*
	(0.078)	(0.078)	(0.092)
Fut.VAT-incr. known, 1 Lag(s)	0.006	0.069	0.143
	(0.081)	(0.107)	(0.111)
Fut.VAT-incr. known, 2 Lag(s)	0.084	0.181	0.225
	(0.128)	(0.142)	(0.153)
Fut.VAT-incr. known, 3 Lag(s)	0.093	0.196	0.302*
	(0.120)	(0.145)	(0.176)
Fut.VAT-incr. known, 4 Lag(s)	0.585	0.522*	2.848
	(0.475)	(0.295)	(1.778)
Fut.VAT-incr. known, 5 Lag(s)	2.285**	2.002*	5.312***
	(1.064)	(1.131)	(1.717)
Periods since last price change, $z(i_n, j, t,)$	0.010	0.054	0.056
	(0.028)	(0.038)	(0.040)
$z(i_n, j, t,)^2$	0.001	0.001	0.001
	(0.001)	(0.001)	(0.001)

Dummy 1st quarter	0.320*	0.299*	0.391*
	(0.180)	(0.179)	(0.208)
Dummy 2nd quarter	0.253	0.284*	0.383**
	(0.172)	(0.171)	(0.169)
Dummy 3rd quarter	0.001	0.040	0.062
	(0.183)	(0.183)	(0.204)
Sales	28.137***	31.733***	29.367***
	(0.618)	(0.627)	(0.621)
Sales end	11.402***	10.868***	10.540***
	(0.760)	(0.744)	(0.749)
Dummy 2000Q2	1.928***	1.895***	1.283***
	(0.304)	(0.314)	(0.414)
Acc.sec.infl., $\pi(i_n, j, t)$		0.019	0.010
		(0.071)	(0.081)
Price relative to mean price, $\rho(i_n, j, t\ \ 1)$		0.158***	0.162***
		(0.013)	(0.013)
$\rho(i_n, j, t\ \ 1)^2$		0.001***	0.001***
		(0.000)	(0.000)
GDP growth, yoy			0.015
			(0.100)
Lag 1 quarters			0.004
			(0.125)
Lag 2 quarters			0.133
			(0.137)
Lag 3 quarters			0.064
			(0.140)
Lag 4 quarters			0.036
			(0.096)
RER index, gr. qoq			0.013
			(0.031)
Lag 1 quarters			0.042
			(0.033)
Lag 2 quarters			0.081**
			(0.034)
Lag 3 quarters			0.032
			(0.036)
Lag 4 quarters			0.051
			(0.039)
3m LIBOR, 1st diff.			0.487*
			(0.259)
Lag 1 quarters			0.399*
			(0.213)
Lag 2 quarters			0.589**
			(0.248)

Lag 3 quarters			0.141
			(0.249)
Lag 4 quarters			0.009
			(0.225)
Pseudo R^2	0.039	0.137	0.147
Observations	29,940	29,940	29,940

Standard errors in parentheses
* $p < 0.1$, ** $p < 0.05$, *** $p < 0.01$

Bibliography

Adjemian, S., Bastani, H., Juillard, M., Karamé, F., Mihoubi, F., Perendia, G., Pfeifer, J., Ratto, M., Villemot, S., 2011. Dynare: Reference manual, version 4. Dynare Working Papers 1, CEPREMAP.

Aghion, P., Farhi, E., Kharroubi, E., 2012. Monetary policy, liquidity, and growth. NBER Working Papers 18072, National Bureau of Economic Research, Inc.

Aghion, P., Howitt, P., 1992. A model of growth through creative destruction. Econometrica 60 (2), 323–351.

Aghion, P., Saint-Paul, G., 1991. On the virtue of bad times: An analysis of the interaction between economic fluctuations and productivity growth. CEPR Discussion Papers 578, CEPR.

Aiyagari, S. R., 1994. Uninsured idiosyncratic risk and aggregate saving. The Quarterly Journal of Economics 109 (3), 659–684.

Altissimo, F., Mojon, B., Zaffaroni, P., 2009. Can aggregation explain the persistence of inflation? Journal of Monetary Economics 56 (2), 231–241.

Álvarez, L. J., Dhyne, E., Hoeberichts, M., Kwapil, C., Bihan, H. L., Lünnemann, P., Martins, F., Sabbatini, R., Stahl, H., Vermeulen, P., Vilmunen, J., 2006. Sticky prices in the Euro area: A summary of new micro-evidence. Journal of the European Economic Association 4 (2-3), 575–584.

Andolfatto, D., 1996. Business cycles and labor-market search. American Economic Review 86 (1), 112–132.

Arkolakis, C., Demidova, S., Klenow, P. J., Rodriguez-Clare, A., 2008. Endogenous variety and the gains from trade. American Economic Review 98 (2), 444–450.

Arrow, K., 1962. The economic implications of learning-by-doing. The Review of Economic Studies 29 (3), 155–173.

Atkeson, A., Burstein, A. T., 2010. Innovation, firm dynamics, and international trade. Journal of Political Economy 118 (3), 433–484.

Atkeson, A., Kehoe, P. J., 2007. Modeling the transition to a new economy: Lessons from two technological revolutions. American Economic Review 97 (1), 64–88.

Barro, R. J., 1990. Government spending in a simple model of endogenous growth. Journal of Political Economy 98 (5), 103–126.

Barro, R. J., Gordon, D. B., 1983. Rules, discretion and reputation in a model of monetary policy. Journal of Monetary Economics 12 (1), 101–121.

Berentsen, A., Waller, C. J., 2009. Optimal stabilization policy with endogenous firm entry. Working Papers 2009-032, Federal Reserve Bank of St. Louis.

Bergin, P. R., Corsetti, G., 2008. The extensive margin and monetary policy. Journal of Monetary Economics 55 (7), 1222–1237.

Bergin, P. R., Glick, R., 2007. Tradability, productivity, and international economic integration. Journal of International Economics 73 (1), 128–151.

Bernanke, B. S., Gertler, M., 2001. Should central banks respond to movements in asset prices? American Economic Review 91 (2), 253–257.

Bernanke, B. S., Gertler, M., Gilchrist, S., 1999. The financial accelerator in a quantitative business cycle framework. In: Taylor, J. B., Woodford, M. (Eds.), Handbook of Macroeconomics. Vol. 1. Elsevier, Ch. 21, pp. 1341–1393.

Bernard, A. B., Eaton, J., Jensen, J. B., Kortum, S., 2003. Plants and productivity in international trade. American Economic Review 93 (4), 1268–1290.

Bernard, A. B., Redding, S. J., Schott, P. K., 2010. Multiple-product firms and product switching. American Economic Review 100 (1), 70–97.

Bhattacharya, J., Haslag, J., Russell, S., 2005. The role of money in two alternative models: When is the friedman rule optimal, and why? Journal of Monetary Economics 52 (8), 1401–1433.

Bilbiie, F. O., Fujiwara, I., Ghironi, F., 2014. Optimal monetary policy with endogenous entry and product variety. Journal of Monetary Economics 64 (1), 1–20.

Bilbiie, F. O., Ghironi, F., Melitz, M., 2007. Monetary policy and business cycles with endogenous entry and product variety. NBER Working Papers 13199, National Bureau of Economic Research, Inc.

Bilbiie, F. O., Ghironi, F., Melitz, M., 2012. Endogenous entry, product variety, and business cycles. Journal of Political Economy 120 (2), 304–345.

Bils, M., Klenow, P. J., 2004. Some evidence on the importance of sticky prices. Journal of Political Economy 112 (5), 947–985.

Blackburn, K., 1999. Can stabilisation policy reduce long-run growth? The Economic Journal 109 (452), 67–77.

Blanchard, O. J., 1997. The medium run. Brookings Papers on Economic Activity 28 (2), 89–158.

Boivin, J., Giannoni, M. P., Mihov, I., 2009. Sticky prices and monetary policy: Evidence from disaggregated US data. American Economic Review 99 (1), 350–384.

Borenstein, S., Rose, N. L., 1994. Competition and price dispersion in the U.S. airline industry. Journal of Political Economy 102 (4), 653–683.

Bouakez, H., Cardia, E., Ruge-Murcia, F. J., 2005. Habit formation and the persistence of monetary shocks. Journal of Monetary Economics 52 (6), 1073–1088.

Broda, C., Weinstein, D., 2007. Product creation and destruction: Evidence and price implications. NBER Working Papers 13041, National Bureau of Economic Research, Inc.

Broda, C., Weinstein, D. E., 2010. Product creation and destruction: Evidence and price implications. American Economic Review 100 (3), 691–723.

Burnside, C., Eichenbaum, M., 1996. Factor-Hoarding and the Propagation of Business-Cycle Shocks. American Economic Review 86 (5), 1154–1174.

Burnside, C., Eichenbaum, M., Rebelo, S., 1993. Labor hoarding and the business cycle. Journal of Political Economy 101 (2), 245–273.

Caballero, R. J., Hammour, M. L., 1994. The cleansing effect of recessions. American Economic Review 84 (5), 1350–1368.

Calvo, G., 1983. Staggered prices in a utility maximizing framework. Journal of Monetary Economics 12 (3), 383–398.

Campbell, J. R., 1998. Entry, exit, embodied technology, and business cycles. Review of Economic Dynamics 1 (2), 371–408.

Cass, D., 1965. Optimum growth in an aggregative model of capital accumulation. The Review of Economic Studies 32 (3), 233–240.

Cecchetti, S. G., 1986. The frequency of price adjustment: A study of the newsstand prices of magazines. Journal of Econometrics 31 (3), 255–274.

Chu, A. C., Cozzi, G., 2014. R&D and economic growth in a cash-in-advance economy. International Economic Review 55 (2), 507–524.

Chugh, S. K., Ghironi, F., 2011. Optimal Fiscal Policy with Endogenous Product Variety. NBER Working Papers 17319, National Bureau of Economic Research, Inc.

Clay, K., Krishnan, R., Wolff, E., 2001. Prices and price dispersion on the web: Evidence from the online book industry. The Journal of Industrial Economics 49 (4), 521–539.

Cogley, T., Nason, J. M., 1995. Output dynamics in real-business-cycle models. American Economic Review 85 (3), 492–511.

Cook, D., 2001. Time to enter and business cycles. Journal of Economic Dynamics and Control 25 (8), 1241–1261.

Darby, M. R., 1975. The financial and tax effects of monetary policy on interest rates. Economic Inquiry 13 (2), 266–276.

Den Haan, W. J., Ramey, G., Watson, J., 2000. Job destruction and propagation of shocks. American Economic Review 90 (3), 482–498.

Devereux, M. B., Head, A. C., Lapham, B. J., 1996. Aggregate fluctuations with increasing returns to specialization and scale. Journal of Economic Dynamics and Control 20 (4), 627–656.

DiCecio, R., 2009. Sticky wages and sectoral labor comovement. Journal of Economic Dynamics and Control 33 (3), 538–553.

Dixit, A., Stiglitz, J., 1977. Monopolistic competition and optimum product diversity. American Economic Review 67 (3), 297–308.

Dotsey, M., King, R. G., Wolman, A. L., 1999. State-dependent pricing and the general equilibrium dynamics of money and output. The Quarterly Journal of Economics 114 (2), 655–690.

Dunne, T., Roberts, M. J., Samuelson, L., 1988. Patterns of firm entry and exit in U.S. manufacturing industries. The RAND Journal of Economics 19 (4), 495–515.

Edmond, C., Veldkamp, L., 2009. Income dispersion and counter-cyclical markups. Journal of Monetary Economics 56 (6), 791–804.

Erceg, C., Henderson, D., Levin, A., 2000. Optimal monetary policy with staggered wage and price contracts. Journal of Monetary Economics 46 (2), 281–313.

Fehr, E., Goette, L., 2005. Robustness and real consequence of nominal wage rigidity. Journal of Monetary Economics 52 (4), 779–804.

Galí, J., 1994. Monopolistic competition, endogenous markups, and growth. European Economic Review 38 (3-4), 748–756.

Galí, J., 2011. The return of the wage phillips curve. Journal of the European Economic Association 9 (3), 436–461.

Galí, J., Hammour, M., 1993. Long run effects of business cycles. Working paper, MIT.

Galí, J., Smets, F., Wouters, R., 2012. Unemployment in an estimated new Keynesian model. NBER Macroeconomics Annual 26 (1), 329–360.

Gerlach, S., Moretti, L., 2011. Monetary policy and TIPS yields before the crisis. CEPR Discussion Papers 8560, CEPR.

Gertler, M., Leahy, J., 2008. A phillips curve with an ss foundation. Journal of Political Economy 116 (3), 533–572.

Golosov, M., Lucas, R. E., April 2007. Menu costa and philips curves. Journal of Political Economy 115 (2), 171–199.

Guerrieri, V., Lorenzoni, G., 2011. Credit crises, precautionary savings, and the liquidity trap. NBER Working Papers 17583, National Bureau of Economic Research, Inc.

Guvenen, F., 2011. Macroeconomics with heterogeneity: A practical guide. NBER Working Papers 17622, National Bureau of Economic Research, Inc.

Hall, R., 2011. The long sump. American Economic Review 101 (2), 431–469.

Hall, R. E., 1988. The relation between price and marginal cost in U.S. industry. Journal of Political Economy 96 (5), 921–947.

Hansen, B. E., 1997. Approximate asymptotic P values for structural-change tests. Journal of Business and Economic Statistics 15 (1), 60–67.

Helpman, E., 2006. Trade, FDI, and the organization of firms. Journal of Economic Literature 44 (3), 589–630.

Hoeberichts, M., Stokman, A., 2011. Price dispersion in Europe: Does the business cycle matter? DNB Working Papers 285, Netherlands Central Bank, Research Department.

Honoré, B. E., Kaufmann, D., Lein, S., 2012. Asymmetries in price-setting behavior: New microeconometric evidence from Switzerland. Journal of Money, Credit and Banking 44 (s2), 211–236.

Hopenhayn, H., Rogerson, R., 1993. Job turnover and policy evaluation: A general equilibrium analysis. Journal of Political Economy 101 (5), 915–938.

Hopenhayn, H. A., 1992. Exit, selection, and the value of firms. Journal of Economic Dynamics and Control 16 (3-4), 621–653.

Howitt, P., 1988. Business cycles with costly search and recruiting. The Quarterly Journal of Economics 103 (1), 147–165.

Huang, K. X. D., Liu, Z., 2002. Staggered price-setting, staggered wage-setting, and business cycle persistence. Journal of Monetary Economics 49 (2), 405–433.

Iacoviello, M., 2005. House prices, borrowing constraints, and monetary policy in the business cycle. American Economic Review 95 (3), 739–764.

IMF, 2014. World economic outlook - Recovery strengthens, Remains uneven. International Monetary Fund.

Jaimovich, N., Floetotto, M., 2008. Firm dynamics, markup variations, and the business cycle. Journal of Monetary Economics 55 (7), 1238–1252.

Jovanovic, B., 1982. Selection and the evolution of industry. Econometrica 50 (3), 649–670.

Kaplan, G., Menzio, G., 2014. The morphology of price dispersion. NBER Working Papers 19877, National Bureau of Economic Research, Inc.

Kashyap, A. K., 1995. Sticky prices: New evidence from retail catalogs. The Quarterly Journal of Economics 110 (1), 245–274.

Kaufmann, D., 2009. Price-setting behaviour in Switzerland: Evidence from CPI micro data. Swiss Journal of Economics and Statistics (SJES) 145 (III), 293–349.

Kaufmann, D., Lein, S. M., 2013. Sticky prices or rational inattention - What can we learn from sectoral price data? European Economic Review 64 (C), 384–394.

King, R. G., Rebelo, S. T., 1999. Resuscitating real business cycles. In: Taylor, J. B., Woodford, M. (Eds.), Handbook of Macroeconomics. Vol. 1. Elsevier, Ch. 14, pp. 927–1007.

Klenow, P. J., Kryvtsov, O., 2008. State-dependent or time-dependent pricing: Does it matter for recent U.S. inflation? The Quarterly Journal of Economics 123 (3), 863–904.

Kongsamut, P., Rebelo, S., Xie, D., 2001. Beyond balanced growth. The Review of Economic Studies 68 (4), 869–882.

Koopmans, T., 1965. On the concept of optimal economic growth. In: delle Scienze, P. A. (Ed.), The econometric approach to development planning. North-Holland, pp. 225–287.

Krugman, P., 1998. It's baaack: Japan's slump and the return of the liquidity trap. Brookings Papers on Economic Activity 29 (2), 137–187.

Lach, S., Tsiddon, D., 1992. The behavior of prices and inflation: An empirical analysis of disaggregated price data. Journal of Political Economy 100 (2), 349–389.

Lein, S. M., 2010. When do firms adjust prices? Evidence from micro panel data. Journal of Monetary Economics 57 (6), 696–715.

Lewis, V., 2009. Business cycle evidence on firm entry. Macroeconomic Dynamics 13 (5), 605–624.

Lewis, V., 2013. Optimal monetary policy and firm entry. Macroeconomic Dynamics 17 (8), 1687–1710.

Maćkowiak, B., Moench, E., Wiederholt, M., 2009. Sectoral price data and models of price setting. Journal of Monetary Economics 56 (Supplement), S78–S99.

Maćkowiak, B., Wiederholt, M., 2009. Optimal sticky prices under rational inattention. American Economic Review 99 (3), 769–803.

Mankiw, N. G., Reis, R., 2002. Sticky information versus sticky prices: A proposal to replace the new Keynesian Phillips curve. The Quarterly Journal of Economics 117 (4), 1295–1328.

Martin, P., Rogers, C. A., 1997. Stabilization policy, learning-by-doing, and economic growth. Oxford Economic Papers 49 (2), 152–166.

Martin, P., Rogers, C. A., 2000. Long-term growth and short-term economic instability. European Economic Review 44 (2), 359–381.

Melitz, M., Redding, S., 2014. New trade models, new welfare implications. Working Paper 65406, Harvard University OpenScholar.

Melitz, M. J., 2003. The impact of trade on intra-industry reallocations and aggregate industry productivity. Econometrica 71 (6), 1695–1725.

Melitz, M. J., Ottaviano, G. I. P., 2008. Market size, trade, and productivity. The Review of Economic Studies 75 (1), 295–316.

Mertens, K., Ravn, M. O., 2011. Leverage and the financial accelerator in a liquidity trap. American Economic Review 101 (3), 413–416.

Merz, M., 1995. Search in the labor market and the real business cycle. Journal of Monetary Economics 36 (2), 269–300.

Mortensen, D. T., Pissarides, C. A., 1994. Job creation and job destruction in the theory of unemployment. The Review of Economic Studies 61 (3), 397–415.

Nakamura, E., Steinsson, J., 2008. Five facts about prices: A reevaluation of menu cost models. The Quarterly Journal of Economics 123 (4), 1415–1464.

Ngo, P. V., 2014. Habit formation in state-dependent pricing models: Implications for the dynamics of output and prices. Economics Letters 123 (3), 336–340.

Ramey, G., Ramey, V. A., 1995. Cross-country evidence on the link between volatility and growth. American Economic Review 85 (5), 1138–1151.

Ramsey, F. P., 1928. A mathematical theory of saving. The Economic Journal 38 (152), 543–559.

Rogoff, K., 1985. The optimal degree of commitment to an intermediate monetary target. The Quarterly Journal of Economics 100 (4), 1169–1189.

Rotemberg, J. J., 1982. Monopolistic price adjustment and aggregate output. The Review of Economic Studies 49 (4), 517–531.

Rotemberg, J. J., Woodford, M., 1992. Oligopolistic pricing and the effects of aggregate demand on economic activity. Journal of Political Economy 100 (6), 1153–1207.

Rotemberg, J. J., Woodford, M., 1996. Real-business-cycle models and the forecastable movements in output, hours, and consumption. American Economic Review 86 (1), 71–89.

Saint-Paul, G., 1993. Productivity growth and the structure of the business cycle. European Economic Review 37 (4), 861–883.

Schaffer, M. E., 2005. Xtivreg2: Stata module to perform extended iv/2sls, gmm and ac/hac, liml and k-class regression for panel data models. Statistical Software Components, Boston College, Department of Economics.

Schmitt-Grohé, S., Uribe, M., 2007. Optimal simple and implementable monetary and fiscal rules. Journal of Monetary Economics 54 (6), 1702–1725.

Schmitt-Grohé, S., Uribe, M., 2012. The making of a great contraction with a liquidity trap and a jobless recovery. NBER Working Papers 18544, National Bureau of Economic Research, Inc.

Schumpeter, J. A., 1939. Business cycles: A theoretical, historical and statistical analysis of the capitalist process. Mc-Graw-Hill.

Sengupta, A., Wiggins, S. N., 2014. Airline pricing, price dispersion, and ticket characteristics on and off the internet. American Economic Journal: Economic Policy 6 (1), 272–307.

Smets, F., Wouters, R., 2007. Shocks and frictions in US business cycles: A bayesian DSGE approach. American Economic Review 97 (3), 586–606.

Solow, R. M., 2000. Toward a macroeconomics of the medium run. Journal of Economic Perspectives 14 (1), 151–158.

Sorensen, A. T., 2000. Equilibrium price dispersion in retail markets for prescription drugs. Journal of Political Economy 108 (4), 833–850.

Strittmatter, A., Sunde, U., 2013. Health and economic development - Evidence from the introduction of public health care. Journal of Population Economics 26 (4), 1549–1584.

Taylor, J. B., 1979. Staggered wage setting in a macro model. American Economic Review 69 (2), 108–113.

Taylor, J. B., 1980. Aggregate dynamics and staggered contracts. Journal of Political Economy 88 (1), 1–23.

Terza, J. V., Basu, A., Rathouz, P. J., 2008. Two-stage residual inclusion estimation: Addressing endogeneity in health econometric modeling. Journal of Health Economics 27 (3), 531–543.

Werning, I., 2011. Managing a liquidity trap: Monetary and fiscal policy. NBER Working Papers 17344, National Bureau of Economic Research, Inc.

MIX
Papier aus verantwortungsvollen Quellen
Paper from responsible sources
FSC® C105338

If you have any concerns about our products,
you can contact us on
ProductSafety@springernature.com

In case Publisher is established outside the EU,
the EU authorized representative is:
Springer Nature Customer Service Center GmbH
Europaplatz 3, 69115 Heidelberg, Germany

Printed by Libri Plureos GmbH
in Hamburg, Germany